BOOK of MORMON
Personalities

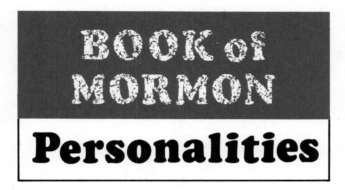

BOOK of MORMON
Personalities

JOSEPH LUNDSTROM

Published by
Deseret Book Company
1972

Second Printing 1972

Library of Congress Catalog Card No. 76-102890
Copyright © 1969
by
Deseret Book Company

Preface

There are 580 names of persons and places in the Book of Mormon. Some are repeated extensively, others only once. All are there for a reason. A great deal can be learned about some of these persons from the Book of Mormon record. Curious speculation is induced by the limited references to others. Of those mentioned only once or twice, often nothing is disclosed. Some of these latter individuals must have been remarkable servants of the Lord, but the record is too limited to show the full personality, and we will have to wait for further enlightenment.

Book of Mormon Personalities first appeared in the *Deseret News* as *Book of Mormon Profiles,* a series on the editorial page of the *Church News.* Of necessity, each Profile was of limited length. Where much information about the individual is recorded—Nephi, son of Lehi, for example—it was necessary to select arbitrarily and choose that which, in the judgment of the writer, best represented the personality and character of the person considered. Students of the Book of Mormon personalities may not agree with one's choice of illustrative materials used for their favorite characters, and this is their right.

Most of the major characters in the Book of Mormon were included in the *Church News* series before it was concluded. There are perhaps other persons who might have been included. Some of the less important individuals were included in the series because there seemed to be within their lives a lesson for readers of today. Of those omitted, readers are invited to write their own sketches. They will find it a profitable, testimony-strengthening experience. All of the Profiles printed in the *Church News* are reprinted here.

The illustrations, drawn by Ronald Crosby, one of Utah's gifted young artists, first appeared in black and white in *The Book of Mormon Story,* by Mary Pratt Parrish. The drawings were adapted for color in the *Church News* by *Deseret News* staff artists, Richard Gregersen and Reed Mc-Gregor. In addition, several of the drawings used in the series and included here were done by Mr. Gregersen (Jacob, David Whitmer, Martin Harris, and Joseph Smith), and Mr. McGregor (Corianton, Helaman II, Nephi II, and Jesus Christ.) Charles Nickerson drew the illustration of Hagoth.

Appreciation is expressed to Mrs. Parrish and Mr. Crosby for use of the illustrations appearing in their book, and to the artists of the *Deseret News* staff for their original work. Gratitude is also expressed to the Deseret News Publishing Company for permission to reprint the Book of Mormon Profiles in book form.

Joseph Lundstrom
September, 1969

Contents

Foreword

The Book of Mormon is a divinely inspired record of ancient peoples inhabiting the Western Hemisphere centuries before and after Christ. The record was kept by prophets of God "—Written by way of commandment and also by the spirit of prophecy and revelation—". Joseph Smith Jr., was given an abridgement of the records by the Angel Moroni who had been the final custodian and had hid it in the Hill Cumorah in western New York shortly before his death about A.D. 421. The record, on plates of gold, was given to Joseph in 1827. By the power of God he translated it into English.

The narrative of the Book of Mormon concerns two peoples who flourished in America as descendants of small colonies divinely guided to the Western Hemisphere from the Near East. One of these groups is called *Jaredites*. The other is known as Nephites—from whom a third dissident group arose, called *Lamanites*. The record is of God's dealings with these people.

The purposes of the Book of Mormon are to bear record of Jesus Christ as the Redeemer of mankind, to teach the saving doctrines of the gospel in their fulness, and to stand as a witness to the world that Joseph Smith was an appointed prophet of the Lord.

The major characters identified in the Book of Mormon are discussed in the following pages. They are generally in the order they appear in the Book of Mormon.

Lehi: Father Of Nations

He was a "visionary" man, he readily admitted; something of a dreamer perhaps.

But he was also a doer, and when disturbed, he, Lehi, father of nations, could speak to others with such power that they trembled before him. So persuasive were his words that he confounded those who opposed him "that they durst not utter against him."

Father Lehi was a patriarch in every sense. He was faithful, he prophesied, he blessed, he led, he preached and taught.

A descendant of Jacob, through Joseph and Manasseh, Lehi was counseled by the Lord to depart from Jerusalem lest he be destroyed with the wicked.

The amazing journey of Lehi and his small flock, from Jerusalem to the Western Hemisphere (they landed near Valparaiso, Chili, said the Prophet Joseph Smith), is the subject of the first 58 pages of the Book of Mormon.

Their travels, trials, troubles, and their successes are written thereon in detail by Lehi's son, Nephi.

Lehi had been diligent in preaching to the unworthy residents of Jerusalem. But they mocked him and sought his life.

Lehi was obedient in following the commandment to depart from Jerusalem with his family. In so doing, he willingly abandoned his house, his gold and silver, and other valuable property.

Lehi lived close to the Lord and was a constant companion of the Spirit, receiving guidance, direction, and glorious manifestations—including a vision of the full history of the world.

Lehi was prayerful, pleading to the Lord for compassion upon his people, and especially his wayward sons, Laman and Lemuel.

Lehi was a grateful man and offered sacrifice in remembrance of his blessings. He rejoiced in his knowledge of God. He sorrowed because of the cruel conduct of his elder sons toward the younger Nephi.

To Lehi we are particularly indebted for several great teachings of the gospel—i.e., explanations of free agency, the Fall of Adam, and the Atonement of Christ:

"Wherefore, the Lord God gave unto man that he should act for himself."

"Adam fell that men might be; and men are, that they might have joy."

Lehi also identifies for us the Western Hemisphere as "a land of promise, a land which is choice above all other lands. . . . And if it so be that they shall serve him according to the commandments which he hath given, it shall be a land of liberty unto them . . ."

Sariah: Mother Of Nations

Sariah is one of the few women identified in the Book of Mormon—five times by name—and the only one about whom there is enough recorded to draw a description.

Sariah is a beautiful Hebrew name. The root is *Sara,* meaning a princess, and *Jah,* or *Iah,* for Jehovah; thus, a princess of Jehovah, an altogether significant name, for like Eve, she also became a mother of nations.

Of Sariah's birth and lineage, the record is blank, as is any reference to her death. She was the wife of Father Lehi, obediently following him from Jerusalem to the Western Hemisphere. She bore six sons and several daughters. The sons were Laman, Lemuel, Nephi, Sam, Jacob, and Joseph.

The four eldest sons were born prior to departure from Jerusalem. Jacob and Joseph were born during the eight-year period the small band of pilgrims journeyed in the wilderness. When the daughters were born is not recorded.

With an attitude normal of any mother and wife, Sariah at times grew discouraged with her husband's leading the family into the wilderness from what was security, position, and wealth.

When the eldest four sons were sent back to Jerusalem for the precious records, Sariah complained aloud to her husband, calling him a dreamer, and accusing him of sending their sons to probable death:

"Behold, thou hast led us forth from the land of our inheritance, and my sons are no more, and we perish in the wilderness."

Lehi admitted to part of her charge:

"I know that I am a visionary man; for if I had not seen the things of God in a vision I should not have known the goodness of God, but had tarried at Jerusalem . . ."

But he comforted Sariah with the words:

"But behold, I have obtained a land of promise, in the which I rejoice; yea, and I know that the Lord will deliver my sons . . . and bring them down again unto us in the wilderness."

When Nephi and his brothers returned "to the tent of my father, behold . . . my mother was comforted."

Her faith in Lehi reassured, Sariah bore testimony to his mission:

"Now I know of a surety that the Lord hath commanded my husband to flee into the wilderness: yea, and I also know of a surety that the Lord hath protected my sons and delivered them . . ."

In a final reference to his mother, Nephi writes that while at sea, his parents were brought down "upon their sick-beds" because of their age and the sorrow and grief they had suffered. However, they lived to reach the Promised Land.

That she must have been an exemplary and faithful daughter of Israel can be concluded from the opening sentence of the Book of Mormon: "I Nephi, having been born of goodly parents . . ."

Laman: A Troublemaker

Stiffnecked! No other word better describes Laman.

He, and his brother Lemuel, the two truculent sons of Lehi and Sariah, were the anguish and sorrow of their parents. Lehi pleaded with Laman, the eldest:

"O that thou mightest be like unto this river, continually running into the fountain of all righteousness!"

And to Lemuel, he said:

"O that thou mightest be like unto this valley, firm and steadfast, and immovable in keeping the commandments of the Lord."

But the two sons would have none of it.

Laman, particularly, seemed to be a troublemaker of the worst kind. Willful, unbelieving, stubborn, he rejected the revelations of his father, and at one point, proposed to murder him.

All this despite instructions to the contrary by angels of Heaven.

Deeply jealous, and ever yielding to his rebellious nature, Laman also sought the life of his younger brother, Nephi, despite the admonition of the Lord that Nephi was to rule over him.

A mark of Nephi's great love for his wayward brothers shows forth in that the more they mistreated him, the more he plead with the Lord for their salvation, and the more he rejoiced when they turned to righteousness—infrequently as it may have been.

Laman married one of the daughters of Ishmael, and from this marriage, presumably, came the royal house which governed the Lamanites.

After arriving in the Western Hemisphere, Laman continued his evil habits. At the death of his father, he again conspired to murder his younger brother. But Nephi, warned by the Lord, separated himself and those who would follow from Laman and his supporters.

Left now without the priesthood, the records which included their genealogies, and the teachings of the Lord, Laman and his people became even more barbaric. Eventually, they became a dark-skinned, degenerate, cruel, and loathsome people, living almost on the level of animals.

Little is known of Lemuel. He appears as a shadow of his elder brother, siding with him in disobedience, joining in the cruel treatment of Nephi, and remaining with Laman when Nephi and his followers departed.

The Book of Mormon record is bare of any descendant of Lemuel who rose to prominence of position or in character.

Nephi: Man Of Faith

"And it came to pass that I, Nephi, said unto my father: I will go and do the things which the Lord hath commanded, for I know that the Lord giveth no commandments unto the children of men, save he shall prepare a way for them . . ."

The lessons in this short passage of scripture from the Book of Mormon (I Nephi 3:7) are many, and are indicative of the great faith of Nephi.

No greater Book of Mormon personality walked the Americas than Nephi, born of "goodly parents" and "taught somewhat in the learning" of his father. He was a prophet of the first rank, of the Lord. His trials were large, but greater still was his zealous devotion to serve God.

A natural leader whose heart overflowed with compassion for his family and friends, Nephi humbly sought divine direction in all that he did.

He was true to his heritage, courageous when confronted with dangers, patient with those who rejected his counsel, and tireless in opposing evil.

Nephi spent much of his life preaching repentance. And yet he was a skilled craftsman. Under the direction of the Lord, he built a ship to carry his father's people to the Western Hemisphere; he fashioned tools, and weapons; taught the women how to take wool of the sheep and fur of llamas and make clothes therefrom, and taught men how to build and farm.

Nephi was a prophet, predicting events to come. He was a revelator, interpreting dreams and making plain the teachings of the Gospel.

Like most of the prophets of the Lord, he stood alone time after time while his brethren—those he loved most— reviled, abused, and persecuted him. And each time he pleaded with them to remove wickedness and hardness from their hearts and to humble themselves before God. Frequently he was successful.

Youthful, but large for his age, he was visited by the Lord and told that because of his faithfulness, he should "be made a ruler and a teacher over thy brethren."

Ever faithful, Nephi was uncomplaining in the face of all his tribulations, and his father, Lehi, said of him, ". . . and thou shalt be favored of the Lord, because thou has not murmured."

Eventually, Nephi was asked to be king over his followers, so loved was he by them. He accepted reluctantly, and successfully led them in battling against the evil followers of his brother, Laman. Succeeding kings were thereafter named Nephi the Second, Nephi the Third, etc., in deference to this great prophet.

Laban: Wicked, Powerful

He was a large man, rich and powerful. He was obstinate. In his heart, he was a murderer. Covetous, he was also a thief.

Yet he associated with the elders of the corrupt Jewish Church, probably because of his inherent right to be custodian of the records containing the law and the genealogies.

He was thoroughly evil, and one night when he was drunk, Nephi slew him.

His name was Laban, and according to the records, he was a descendent of Joseph who was sold into Egypt.

Much about Laban is unknown: How he came to have the records? What his position in the worldly Jewish Church was? How a descendent of Joseph came to be living a life of influence in Jerusalem when he should properly have been with the Northern Kingdom of Israel? These are intriguing questions.

But Laban did have the records. And because they contained much that was necessary for Lehi and his people to know, the law and the genealogies, lest they "should dwindle and perish in unbelief," Lehi sent his four sons, Laman, Lemuel, Nephi, and Sam, after them.

Arriving at the city, the four drew lots, and it fell to Laman to go before the powerful Laban and ask for the Brass Plates.

But the wicked Israelite refused to give the records and drove Laman from his presence, even trying to kill him. Laman, however, escaped and returned to his brothers.

Nephi next suggested that they go to their former home and take of the riches that their father had left behind, and use this to buy the records from Laban.

The offer was rejected again, and Laban lusted after the gold and silver and other precious things that were offered him. He sent his servants to slay the four sons of Lehi: in their flight, they had to abandon their father's wealth.

Finally, Nephi went alone into the city, and guided by the spirit, found Laban drunken with wine. Withdrawing Laban's sword and instructed by heaven, Nephi cut off Laban's head.

"Behold the Lord slayeth the wicked to bring forth his righteous purposes. It is better that one man should perish than that a nation should dwindle and perish in unbelief," Nephi was told.

Then dressing himself in Laban's clothes, Nephi went to Laban's house and ordered the servant to open the treasury from which the Brass Plates were secured.

When the plates were delivered to Lehi, and he read them, "he was filled with the spirit . . ." Nephi wrote ". . . they were desirable; yea, even of great worth unto us, insomuch that we could preserve the commandments of the Lord unto our children."

Zoram: Laban's Servant

The history of Zoram, the servant of Laban, is sparse, but of special interest because it adds important details to the history of Father Lehi's little band of pilgrims.

Nephi and his three brothers returned to Jerusalem with a specific assignment from their father to obtain the Brass Plates from Laban—records very important to Lehi because they contained an official scripture of the House of Israel.

Nephi acquired the precious records by deceiving Zoram. Dressed in the slain Laban's armor, Nephi went to the dead man's residence and in the voice of Laban, ordered Zoram to bring the Brass Plates. Being night, Zoram thought it was his master, and having the keys, opened the treasury.

Nephi then ordered Zoram to follow him "to my elder brethren," and the servant, thinking this meant the elders and priests of the Jews, obeyed.

However, Nephi meant his own brothers secretly waiting outside the walls of the city. When the two men arrived at the hiding place, Nephi's brothers were frightened, believing it was Laban. They feared their brother had been killed, that Laban was coming now to slay them, and they fled.

The brothers stopped their flight, however, when Nephi called out to them in his own voice. Now it was Zoram's turn to be alarmed because he thought he had been following his master.

Zoram attempted to flee, but Nephi seized him and quickly explained his mission and the necessity for possessing the records. Zoram was promised freedom and safety if he would swear to remain with Nephi and his brothers. This Zoram promised with an oath, and Nephi writes that his fears "did cease concerning him."

Oath-making was a practice steeped in tradition and honor. An oath once sincerely given was a firm bond of trust. Both Zoram and Nephi understood this and thereafter had full faith in each other.

Accompanying Nephi into the wilderness to the camp of Lehi, Zoram became a fully accepted member of the group. He married the eldest daughter of Ishmael. Shortly before his death, Lehi gave Zoram a father's blessing in the same manner he blessed his own sons, promising:

". . . and I know that thou art a true friend unto my son, Nephi, forever. Wherefore, because thou hast been faithful thy seed shall be blessed with his seed, that they dwell in prosperity long upon the face of this land. . . ."

The name *Zoram,* from Hebrew, takes its root in *Zur,* meaning rock, and symbolizes stability, reliability and firmness.

Of the remainder of Zoram's life the record is blank. However, several important men in later Nephite history, Amalickiah and Ammaron for example, are identified as his descendants.

Ishmael Was Faithful

For a season, Lehi and his family had been in the wilderness. But the Lord instructed Lehi it was not proper for them to be alone, and that his sons should return to the land of Jerusalem and "bring down Ishmael and his family into the wilderness."

Accordingly, Nephi and his brothers returned to Jerusalem, to the house of Ishmael where they "did gain favor" and were able to tell Ishmael of the teachings of the Lord to their father. Ishmael's heart was softened, and he and his household journeyed into the wilderness to join Lehi.

Ishmael's relationship is not explained in Nephi's writings. The account takes him for granted, unlike other personalities who are identified; this has led some scholars to suggest that Ishmael may have been closely related to Lehi.

Whatever the case, Ishmael and his family were ready to listen to Nephi explain the Lord's desires concerning them and accepted the invitation to join Lehi in the desert.

The journey was troublesome. Nephi's two elder brothers, Laman and Lemuel, two of Ishmael's daughters, two of his sons, and their families, rebelled against continuing the trip, and sought to return to their home in Jerusalem.

Nephi rebuked the murmurers and upbraided Laman and Lemuel. As his elders, they ought to be setting a proper example for the others, Nephi said.

The scolding angered the two brothers, and they seized Nephi and tied him with cords, "for they sought to take away my life, that they might leave me in the wilderness to be devoured by wild beasts."

But Nephi, praying mightily to the Lord, burst his bonds and again stood before his brethren, remonstrating them. They were angry yet, and would have seized him a second time, but the wife of Ishmael, one of her daughters and a son "did plead with my brethren insomuch that they did soften their hearts, and they did cease striving to take away my life," writes Nephi.

The journey continued without further incident until the party reached the tents of Lehi where there was rejoicing and thanksgiving at the safe arrival.

Ishmael's eldest daughter married Zoram, the servant of Laban, and four other daughters married Lehi's sons.

According to a discourse by Erastus Snow in Logan, Utah, May 6, 1882, Ishmael was a descendant of Ephraim, while Nephi was of the lineage of Manassah. The Prophet Joseph Smith is cited as the source of information.

Although the history is void of further information about Ishmael except his death, presumably he remained faithful and obedient. When the travelers reached a place they named Nahom, Ishmael died and was buried. This brought heavy grief to his family and caused renewed complaint and dissent in the colony.

Jacob Remains Faithful

For Sherem, it would have been better had he never found Jacob.

Sherem was an apostate Nephite, clever in speech, the first in the Book of Mormon to deny Christ would come to redeem mankind.

The wicked Sherem sought out Jacob, the younger brother of Nephi, to turn this great prophet from righteousness.

But Jacob was not to be swayed in his testimony of the Savior: ". . . for I had truly seen angels, and they had ministered unto me. And also, I had heard the voice of the Lord speaking unto me in very word, from time to time; wherefore, I could not be shaken."

After hearing Jacob's testimony of the Christ, Sherem demanded proof. "Show me a sign," he said.

Jacob demurred, for he desired not to tempt God. But he placed the decision in the hands of the Lord, whereupon Sherem was promptly struck down. Before dying, he confessed that he had been wrong.

As a result of his demonstration of the power of God, the Nephites repented of their waywardness, and "peace and the love of God was restored again among the people, and they searched the scriptures, and hearkened no more to the words of this wicked man."

To Jacob we are indebted for many oustanding teachings of the Gospel, notably on the reality of the Savior. As with Nephi, he talked to the Lord on His coming to earth, on His sufferings, and the infinite atonment. Jacob wrote of the need for the resurrection. On the importance of learning, he said:

"O the vainness, and the frailties, and the foolishness of men! When they are learned they think they are wise, and they hearken not unto the counsel of God, for they set it aside, supposing they know of themselves, wherefore their wisdom is foolishness and it profiteth them not.

"But to be learned is good if they hearken unto the counsels of God."

Charged by Nephi at his death to be the spiritual leader of the people, Jacob was sober and humble. He shrank from testifying to the people about their wickedness, lest he offend the ears of the righteous.

Filled with love and compassion, Jacob gave us a beautiful statement on the proper use of wealth and the attitude we should have toward the less fortunate:

"Think of your brethren like unto yourselves, and be familiar with all and free with your substance, that they may be rich like unto you.

"But before ye seek for riches, seek ye for the kingdom of God."

Like his father, Lehi, and Nephi, Jacob was valiant in his witness of the Gospel of Christ. He was a powerful spiritual character, sincere and diligent in teaching the truth.

Enos' Sins Are Forgiven

Enos was at least persevering and persistent.

He was the third in a direct line of father to son who witnessed the Redeemer. Father Lehi, Jacob, and then Enos, each testified of this event in their lives, as did Nephi.

Each son, in turn, paid tribute that he had been taught "in the language of my father," and in the "nurture and admonition of the Lord."

So profoundly impressive was this teaching, that each son sought for himself to know of the reality of Jesus.

The short, but choice, single chapter of the Book of Enos details one of the most impressive lessons to be learned from scripture:

That a genuinely worthy individual who is steadfast in seeking God will find him.

Of his own wondrous experience, Enos writes:

"Behold, I went to hunt beasts in the forests; and the words which I had often heard my father speak concerning eternal life, and the joy of the saints, sunk deep into my heart.

"And my soul hungered; and I kneeled down before my Maker, and I cried unto him in mighty prayer and supplication for mine own soul; and all the day long did I cry unto him; yea, and when the night came I did still raise my voice high that it reached the heavens.

"And there came a voice unto me, saying, Enos, thy sins are forgiven thee, and thou shalt be blessed."

One can only wonder what would have occurred had Enos cut short his prayers before the Lord manifested Himself.

In any event, Enos was filled with a zealous, unshakable faith in the Lord. Having obtained forgiveness for himself, he appealed to God for the salvation of the Nephites—and if that was not possible, that at least a record of them be preserved.

In addition, so great was his compassion that Enos pleaded with the Lord to save the Lamanites—the bloodthirsty enemies of the Nephites.

Enos, having been "Wrought upon by the power of God," spent his life preaching and prophesying unto his people, declaring "the word according to the truth which is in Christ."

Enos rejoiced in these labors, even "above that of the world."

So great was his faith and assurance of salvation because of his diligence that when his life drew to a close, he wrote:

". . . I rejoice in the day when my mortal shall put on immortality and shall stand before Him; then shall I see his face with pleasure, and he will say unto me: Come unto me, ye blessed, there is a place prepared for you in the mansions of my father."

Mosiah: A Key Figure

All that is known about King Mosiah is recorded in eleven paragraphs in the Book of Omni. Much that is important in his life—and to the complete record—is left to imagination.

Yet, Mosiah must have been a person of major significance and is certainly a key figure. Following him is a history of the united Nephites and Mulekites.

Mosiah, living in the land of Nephi, was warned by the Lord—for what reason we know not—to gather the righteous together and depart.

Obedient, Mosiah followed the Lord's command, and the people were "led by many preachings and prophesyings.

And they were admonished continually by the word of God; and they were led by the power of his arm, through the wilderness. . ."

Eventually, Mosiah and his people came upon a city and people completely unknown to them—both called *Zarahemla,* after one of their leaders.

The Zarahemla people were exceedingly numerous, crude, half-civilized, war-like. They had brought no records with them but they were led by the Lord from Jerusalem at the time of King Zedekiah, and their language had become corrupted.

These same people, sometimes called *Mulekites,* after Mulek, who was a son of Zedekiah, also denied the Lord.

Mosiah saw that they were taught the language of the Nephites so that the two peoples could understand one another. Soon Mosiah was named king of the combined peoples.

The Mulekites rejoiced when the Nephites discovered them because of the written records—histories, genealogies, and scriptures—that Mosiah and his followers brought with them.

The people of Zarahemla brought to Mosiah a large engraved stone, "and he did interpret the engravings by the gift and power of God." The inscriptions gave a history of the Jaredites and their last surviving king, Coriantumr, who lived with the Mulekites for "nine moons" before he died.

What happened to the Nephites from whom Mosiah separated is unrecorded. Years later, when Zeniff and a group from Zarahemla returned to the "land of their inheritance," they found it occupied by Lamanites and the cities in disrepair. Presumably, the Nephites were destroyed as had been prophesied by an earlier prophet, Jacob.

Whatever their fortune, the remainder of the Book of Mormon, from Omni 12 to the end (Ether excepted) is the history of Mosiah's smaller group of Nephites united with the Mulekites.

Of Mosiah's personal history, his reign, and influence, the record is blank. He was, of course, a righteous leader and when he died was succeeded by his son, Benjamin, who became the third generation to reign righteously over the people.

Benjamin: A Holy Man

He was old and weary, and it was time to pass the royal mantle of kingship to another.

He had fought the enemies of righteousness with the Sword of Laban and brought peace to Zarahemla once more. He was, wrote Mormon, a holy man who ruled justly.

But now his days were countable, and he was impressed to address again his beloved people among whom he had labored so many years with his own hands.

King Benjamin had his son, Mosiah, assemble the people at the temple. They were too numerous for all to enter, however, so he had erected a tower and preached to them from it. (His oration is the only formal speech recorded in the Book of Mormon.) However, not everyone could hear even then so he directed his words to be written and circulated.

These words mark King Benjamin as one of the noble and great spirits of the earth. His teachings, outlined in his remarkable sermon, are sublime, worthy of emulation by all. His words are simple, sincere, warm, yet dignified. They are forceful and persuasive.

Three major themes were taught by the king:

One, that "when ye are in the service of your fellow beings, ye are only in the service of your God."

Two, that an angel had appeared to him with "tidings of great joy," which he was instructed to share with the people. The message was of the Savior, His coming to earth, His death, resurrection, and the effects of the atonement.

Three, a testimony of the Savior was given by King Benjamin, along with counsel to be obedient, to believe in God, His wisdom, power, greatness, and goodness. Practical advice was given to parents to care for their children, to teach them to "walk in the ways of truth and soberness," and to love and serve one another.

Benjamin reminded his listeners to remember the beggar and the poor—for all are beggars and poor before the Lord—to be diligent, and to continue in faith.

So forceful was his magnificent sermon that the people fell down in awe and humility, and cried for the mercy of God that they might be forgiven through the atoning sacrifice of Christ.

King Benjamin blessed his people and told them to take upon themselves the name of Christ and remain true to the covenants which they made.

The wise king made a roll of those who so covenanted, and "there was not one soul . . . but who had entered into the covenant and taken upon them the name of Christ."

Benjamin then consecrated his son, Mosiah, to be king and ruler over the people, and appointed priests to teach them, "to stir them up in remembrance of the oath which they had made. . . ."

After Mosiah began his rule, Benjamin lived three more years, revered and loved by his people.

Zeniff Leads Expedition

In the days of King Benjamin, two parties went out from Zarahemla to find the land of their forefathers. The first group failed, and the second did not return. Zeniff was a member of both groups.

Zeniff explains that he was "over-zealous to inherit the land of our fathers . . ." He had labored as a spy in the first effort, but finding "good" among the Lamanites, desired that they should not be destroyed. This brought contention in the party; they quarreled and fought, and only a few lived to return to Zarahemla.

On the second expedition, Zeniff, now the leader, and his people become lost and suffered from famine and assorted trials. The people generally were neglectful of their duties to the Lord. After many days they reached the land of Lehi-Nephi, the home of their forebears. But it was occupied by Lamanites.

Zeniff entered into an agreement with the Lamanite king, a traitorous man named Laman, who pretended to be friendly. His real intent, however, was to make Zeniff and his followers slaves of the slothful and lazy Lamanites. Laman gave Zeniff and his party the lands of Lehi-Nephi and Shilom.

Finding the cities in disrepair and crumbling, Zeniff taught his people to be industrious and soon they began to prosper and grow rapidly in numbers. King Laman feared his own people would shortly become the weaker of the two peoples, so he began to stir up his subjects and in the thirteenth year, the Lamanites suddenly and unexpectedly attacked the Nephites.

Quickly Zeniff armed his people with weapons, but he had prepared them also in righteousness, and in the strength of the Lord they went out to defend themselves. Led personally by Zeniff, the Nephites soundly defeated Laman and his warriors. Peace was restored and lasted twenty-two years.

During this peaceful era, Zeniff taught the Nephites to be even more industrious. Men were taught to till the ground and raise fruits and grains; the women learned to spin and make cloth.

Eventually King Laman died, and was succeeded by his ambitious son, also named Laman, who promptly organized an army to make war on the Nephites. But again, Zeniff, now an old man, rallied his people, and in the strength of their God they destroyed so many Lamanites that the Nephites did not bother to count the dead. Despite his age, Zeniff personally led his army in the victory.

Peace was restored again, and Zeniff, now sensing his life was nearly over, appointed as his successor, his unworthy son Noah.

Back in Zarahemla, when Mosiah succeeded his father, King Benjamin, he sent an expedition in search of Zeniff and his people. Eventually they were found and reunited with the main body of Nephites at Zarahemla.

Noah: A Wicked King

If ever a man deserved the appellation "wicked," it was King Noah, who ruled as second king of the Nephites.

Noah's hand was oppressive, his reign cruel, and his personal behavior vile. Wicked King Noah was a despot in every sense of the word.

Guilty of every kind of sin, Noah gathered around him men of his own ilk, as corrupt and evil as himself, men filled with cowardice and deceit.

Taxing the people of Lehi-Nephi one fifth of all their possessions, Noah beautified the temple, then befouled it with his debaucheries. He himself built a magnificent palace and raised other costly buildings, all at the expense of his subjects.

Shortly after he became monarch, small raiding bands of Lamanites began to harass the Nephites, stealing their flocks, and Noah sent his armies to drive the marauders off. These token victories made the king and his soldiers boastful, and they acquired a lust to shed Lamanite blood.

Now, mature in their sins, the king and his court were warned by the Prophet Abinadi to repent or be destroyed. So far gone in evil were Noah and his priests, however, that they rejected Abinadi's admonition and instead, burned him to death for his teachings regarding the Godhead.

Finally, the people grew weary of Noah's tyranny and depravity, and one of his officers, Gideon, sought to slay the king.

But the cunning ruler fled to the tower near the temple from where he saw an invading Lamanite army. He plead for his life, and then ordered his people to flee.

When the pursuing Lamanites caught the Nephites, the cowardly Noah commanded his men to abandon their women and children to the Lamanites and continue their flight.

Some obeyed, but some did not.

Among those who did flee, shame for their weakhearted behavior eventually overcame their fear. They resolved to return and meet the Lamanites to avenge the slaughter of their families—or die in the attempt.

When depraved Noah objected to his being abandoned, the soldiers' anger arose, and they seized the king and burned him to death.

Thus was a prophecy by Abinadi fulfilled:

"Behold, even as ye have done unto me, so shall it come to pass . . . ye shall be smitten on every hand and shall be driven and scattered to and fro, even as a wild flock is driven by wild and ferocious beasts. And in that day ye shall be hunted, and ye shall be taken by the hand of your enemies, and then shall ye suffer, as I suffer, the pains of death by fire."

Abinadi Warns Noah

He was a strange man, not content to leave well enough alone.

Abinadi was his name. He went among the people of King Noah, warning that the Lord was displeased with their behavior. Unless they repented, the stern prophet said, they would fall into the hands of their enemies, be taken into captivity, and should be sorely afflicted.

Who is this, that should pass judgment upon me and my people? demanded the evil-minded king. But when the people sought to slay Abinadi, the Lord delivered him out of their hands.

Still the people continued their sinful living, and after two years, Abinadi came among them again, this time in disguise, and repeated his warning that unless they would turn from their idolatry, riotous living, and lusting, they would be destroyed.

Abinadi permitted himself to be captured, and King Noah cast him in prison. Soon he was brought before the wicked priests whom the king had appointed to sustain him in his evil.

The priests and guards called Abinadi mad and sought to harm him, but he had not yet delivered the message the Lord had entrusted him to give, and he warned:

"Touch me not, for God shall smite you if ye lay your hands upon me . . ."

And the people of King Noah "durst not lay their hands upon him, for the Spirit of the Lord was upon him . . ."

Abinadi delivered his great and precious message:

"God himself shall come down among the children of men and shall redeem his people. And because he dwelleth in the flesh he shall be called the son of God . . . and thus God breaketh the bands of death, having gained the victory over death . . . teach them that redemption cometh through Christ the Lord . . ."

Once again the people rejected the message, and King Noah, in one final demand, told Abinadi to deny his testimony or die:

". . . for this cause thou shalt be put to death unless thou wilt recall the words thou has spoken evil concerning me and my people."

Abinadi answered, "I will not . . . for they are true."

Alma, a young man, believed Abinadi, and pleaded with the depraved ruler for Abinadi's life, but Noah and his priests were not to be deterred. Alma was driven from their midst, and Abinadi, obedient servant of the Lord, though it cost him his life, was burned at the stake.

". . . and he would not deny the commandments of God," and sealed the truth of his words by his death. His predictions of what would happen to Noah and his people were fulfilled.

Amulon: Crafty and Sadistic

The craftiness of Amulon was exceeded only by his sadistic brutality.

As one of the degenerate priests of the evil King Noah, Amulon probably took part in the slaying of the Prophet Abinadi. When Noah, also was burned to death by his savage subjects, his evil priests fled into the wilderness lest they also die by fire.

The priests, led by Amulon, were ashamed of their behavior, but they were even more frightened of the righteous Nephites, and hid in the wilds, declining even from returning to their wives and children.

After a period of time, the priests discovered a group of daughters of the Lamanites who gathered to "sing and dance and make themselves merry." Lonely, evil, and without wives, Amulon and his followers seized twenty-four of these young women and carried them into the wilderness.

When the Lamanites discovered the women missing, they believed the people of Limhi had captured them and went to war against Limhi and his people—despite an oath between the Nephite and Lamanite rulers to respect each other. When it was discovered that Limhi and his followers were innocent, the fighting ceased.

Meanwhile, Amulon and his associates made wives of the Lamanite women and settled in the land called after the sinful leader. Here they were discovered by Lamanite soldiers. Amulon and his followers and their wives pleaded with such urgency that their lives were spared.

The cunning Amulon and his band joined the Lamanites, and the king, called Laman, appointed Amulon to rule the land of Amulon, and Helam, where Alma the Elder and his followers resided.

Amulon became overseer of Alma's people, and recognized Alma as a dissenter from the original group of priests who had been in Noah's service. Amulon's true character now became more evident. He "began to exercise authority over Alma and his brethren, and began to persecute him, and caused that his children should persecute their children."

So great were the persecutions and burdens that Alma's people began to "cry mightily to God" for deliverance.

Amulon ordered the Nephites to cease their praying upon pain of death, and set guards to watch them.

But Alma and his people "did pour out their hearts to him (God); and he did know the thoughts of their hearts" and relieved their burdens.

Eventually, Alma and his followers escaped from Amulon's tormenting and made their way back to Zarahemla. After this, nothing more is recorded of Amulon.

Limhi: Tributary Monarch

Limhi was a "tributary monarch"—so described as such in the Book of Mormon—because he ruled over the Nephites at the pleasure of the Lamanites.

A son of the depraved King Noah, Limhi was called a "just man."

When the Lamanites captured the Nephites, rather than destroy them, the Lamanites entered into an agreement, permitting the Nephites to possess their lands, but in return, exacting a heavy tribute of half their properties and half of all they produced.

This bondage had been prophesied by the courageous Prophet Abinadi, who warned that unless the people ceased their abominations and repented in sackcloth and ashes, they would be delivered into the hands of their enemies.

So heavy and oppressive did the Lamanite yoke become that three times the Nephites rebelled—with disastrous results—losing many lives in the process. After each abortive try, the Lamanites inflicted heavier punishment and crueler abuses.

Finally, realizing their freedom was in God's hands, the people turned with sorrowful hearts to heaven's way. But the Lord was slow to respond, for He will not be mocked. Only after considerable time did He soften the hearts of the Lamanites that they began to treat their captives with less heavy burdens.

Meanwhile, King Limhi secretly sent a small expedition of men from the city to search for Zarahemla and their Nephite friends.

The expedition wandered in a direction away from Zarahemla and came upon the remains of the destroyed Jaredite nation. They found the twenty-four plates of gold which told of this people, but they were unable to read or translate the records which they delivered to King Limhi.

At the same time, the king was especially mindful of the conditions of his people, recognizing that because of the disastrous wars, many widows and orphans suffered. He kept his people together and ordered the men to impart of their substance to succor the poor from starvation. The concern of Limhi marks him as a compassionate, thoughtful leader.

Eventually, Limhi and his people were located by a small band of sixteen men sent from Zarahemla by King Mosiah. They were led by Ammon, who had been sent to find what had happened to those who had left Zarahemla with Zeniff, Limhi's grandfather.

By careful planning, Limhi, Ammon, and a general called Gideon, lured the Lamanite guards into drunkenness and the Nephites escaped to join with Mosiah's people in Zarahemla where they were taught the gospel and baptized. Nothing further is recorded about King Limhi.

Alma: Influential Leader

Of such majestic character and influential leadership was Alma that he was given the privilege and responsibility to "found" the Church in his day.

So potent was Alma's work that those who followed him "became the children of God."

Alma, called the elder to distinguish from his Paul-like missionary son who bore his father's name, was a youthful priest serving evil King Noah when his heart was pierced by the teachings of the Prophet Abinadi.

Sorely repentant, Alma sought and received from the Lord forgiveness, and promptly began teaching the Nephites the Gospel. But the wicked king drove Alma and his followers into the wilderness.

Several hundred believers gathered around Alma and he organized them into a church and, "having authority from God," he taught them the true principles of Christianity:

". . . that there should be no contention one with another . . . having their hearts knit together in unity and in love . . .

". . . that they should observe the sabbath day . . . set apart that they should gather themselves together . . . to worship the Lord their God . . .

". . . that the people of the church should impart of their substance, every one according to that which he had . . . and they did walk uprightly before God, imparting to one another both temporally and spiritually according to their needs and wants."

In such esteem did the people hold Alma that they urged him to be their king. But he declined, noting the dangers unrighteous kingship could cause.

Returning to Zarahemla after Noah's death, Alma was given full spiritual leadership to establish branches of the Church in the land, and he became high priest for the entire nation.

Traveling from city to city, he taught the Gospel, counseling the people in their duties, reproving their waywardness, and comforting the sorrowful.

One of the dramatic chapters of all the Book of Mormon (Mosiah 27) relates the conversion of the younger Alma who, with the four sons of the king, had become an unholy influence throughout the land.

An angel appeared to them and ordered a halt to their rebellion against the Church. The elder Alma rejoiced at this intercession of heaven—indicative of his great faith.

An obedient minister to the end of his days, Alma received power from on high to commission others to follow him in the work of building the kingdom of God on earth. For this, Alma's name was held in remembrance by the Nephites.

The character of Alma is marked by total faith. He loved righteousnes, the Lord, the souls of men, and liberty. He was a humble, courageous servant of God.

Miracle Of Zeezrom

Raising Zeezrom from his bed of affliction was a miracle; of that the people of Sidom had little doubt.

Alma simply took the tortured and pained Zeezrom by the hand and asked: "Believest thou in the power of Christ unto salvation?"

Zeezrom answered, "Yea, I believe all the words that thou has taught."

With that, Alma cried to the Lord to have mercy upon Zeezrom and heal him according to his faith in Christ.

Immediately, Zeezrom leaped to his feet and began to walk; and the miracle of the healing was told all over Sidom.

Zeezrom had come to Sidon from the sin-wracked city of Ammonihah from where he had been driven with the faithful who believed in the teachings of the Prophet Alma and his companion, Amulek.

Ammonihah was ripe in evil, filled with cunning lawyers who made their livelihood by stirring up the residents to contentions and rioting.

Zeezrom was just such a lawyer—recognized as one of the most clever—and seeking to gain fame and make Alma and Amulek appear foolish by contradicting themselves, he challenged them with questions concerning God.

Alma and Amulek, however, saw through his craftiness, accused him of deceit, and declared the truth to him and his followers.

Because of the two men's perception, the sinful lawyer was shocked and became fearful and began to tremble. As they continued to preach the gospel to the people, Zeezrom became convinced that he was the one who was wrong, and he cried out:

"Behold, I am guilty, and these men are spotless before God."

But the people were angry with Alma and Amulek and reviled Zeezrom, accusing him of being possessed of the devil. The two preachers were cast into prison, but those who believed them, including Zeezrom, fled for their lives.

Zeezrom, fearful that Alma and Amulek would die because of his wicked attempt to ensnare them, became ill with shame and sorrow—so much so that he became "exceedingly sore."

The Lord, however, delivered the two missionaries. They escaped from Ammonihah, made their way to Sidom, found Zeezrom in torment, and raised him from his bed.

From thenceforth, the repentant lawyer used his energy in preaching the message of salvation. His skills, wisdom, and talents were used in building up the kingdom of God. He labored fearlessly as a teacher of righteousness under Alma's direction, doing much good as a missionary to make up for the harm he had caused.

Mosiah II: A Good King

Mosiah II can be called the good king, for he was an exceptional man and ruler, and under him the Nephites lived in peace and plenty, and were a righteous, obedient people.

Mosiah, moreover, was not just a good man and wise ruler, but also he was a prophet and seer and had in his possession the sacred records and the "interpreter" (Urim and Thummim) that he used to translate the twenty-four gold plates that gave the history of the Jaredites—found by the people of King Limhi who had been brought back to the main body of Nephites at Zarahemla.

King Mosiah was a son of King Benjamin, who was a son of the first King Mosiah. But the four sons of Mosiah II refused the kingship, desiring instead to serve as missionaries. This gave the king two concerns, first the safety of his sons—they desired to go to preach to the Lamanites—and who would succeed him on the throne.

On this latter point, the king's worry was that if another man was named king, perhaps at some future date, one of his own sons would claim the throne and that might create havoc.

So Mosiah proposed to his subjects that he remain king until his death, after which the Nephites would be governed by judges elected by themselves.

Mosiah explained that even righteous kings have difficulties and troubles in ruling, and said, this ought not to be, "but that the burden should come upon all the people, that every man might bear his part."

He also warned of the dangers of having an unrighteous king, of the iniquities, abominations, wars, contentions, bloodshed, and stealing that could rise under a wicked ruler.

To his proposal for judges, the people consented, and "they assembled themselves together in bodies throughout the land to cast in their voices concerning who should be their judges, to judge them according to the law which had been given them; and they were exceedingly rejoiced because of the liberty which had been granted unto them."

For his wise leadership and judicial counsel, as well as for spiritual guidance and administration, the people revered King Mosiah:

"And they did wax strong in love towards Mosiah: yea, they did esteem him more than any other man; for they did not look upon him as a tyrant who was seeking for gain, yea, for that lucre which doth corrupt the soul; for he had not exacted riches of them, neither had he delighted in the shedding of blood; but he had established peace in the land, and he had granted unto his people that they should be delivered from all manner of bondage; therefore they did esteem him, yea, exceedingly, beyond measure."

Ammon: A Missionary

Ammon was a missionary. Sorry for the harm he had caused the Church when he was a wayward young man, he was zealous in his determination to make amends.

As one of the four sons of King Mosiah, he felt impressed to go to the Lamanites and teach them the Gospel. But the Nephites scorned the idea. Lamanites cannot be converted, they laughed.

Even the king had doubts, but he sought assurances from the Lord and received counsel that the four young men would be protected.

The missionary effort lasted fourteen years and was highly

successful. Ammon's experience in converting the Lamanite King Lamoni is a moving story of fellowshiping.

The consequences of the missionary work was of such magnitude that Ammon and his bretheren converted thousands of Lamanites, one group even taking upon themselves the name of Ammon, their teacher-missionary, and thereafter were called Ammonites.

Arriving first in a land called Ishmael, Ammon offered to become a servant of the king. Finding favor with the royal household, Ammon, through divine guidance, was able to convert many and organize the Church among the people of Ishmael.

Through his faith, patience, and humility, he led the Gospel-loving Lamanites to the land of Zarahemla where the Nephites set apart the land of Jershon for them as their inheritance. Ammon established his own home among these people and became their presiding officer.

So peace-loving were the Ammonites, because of the influence of this great missionary, that they foreswore the bearing of arms and even war to defend themselves.

So great was their faith and understanding, because of Ammon's teachings, that when Korihor, an unbeliever, came among them, they rejected him completely.

Because of his success as a missionary, this good man expressed unusual gratitude to God for making him and his brothers "instruments in the hands of God to bring about this great work."

Accused of boasting, he said: "I do not boast in my own strength, nor in my own wisdom . . . I know that I am nothing; as to my strength I am weak; therefore I will not boast of myself, but I will boast of my God, for in his strength I can do all things; yea, behold, many mighty miracles we have wrought in this land, for which we will praise his name forever."

If this be boasting, said Ammon, "even so will I boast; for this is my life and my light, my joy and my salvation, and my redemption . . ."

Loving missionary work as he did, it is not surprising to find Ammon, in later years of his life, accompanying Alma in the remarkable mission to the Zoramites.

Aaron: Great Missionary

Aaron had seen an angel of the Lord who told him that he must stop persecuting the Church. So impressive was this message that Aaron put everything else aside to devote the remainder of his life to preaching the Gospel.

With his brothers, Ammon, Amner, Himni, and the younger Alma, Aaron was secretly going about trying to destroy the Church when the angel appeared before them, and with a voice of thunder, warned that they must cease their evil ways.

So deeply impressed were the five young men that never again did they oppose the Lord's work. The four sons of the king instead requested permission to go and preach to the Lamanites.

King Mosiah, concerned about a successor to his throne, asked the people who should be their next ruler. They favored Aaron, but he declined the honor. His brothers in similar fashion refused the throne, and Mosiah was compelled to change the government from a monarch to rule by judges.

When Aaron and his brothers asked to go to the Lamanites, Mosiah feared for their lives, and so inquired of God whether they should go. The answer, from heaven, was:

"Let them go up, for many shall believe on their words, and they shall have eternal life; and I will deliver thy sons out of the hands of the Lamanites."

Chapters 17 to 26 of the Book of Alma give an account of the missionary labors of these brothers and of the extraordinary experiences they had in converting Lamanite kings and their people during a fourteen-year period.

Aaron's missionary efforts began in a city called Jerusalem, controlled by apostate Nephites. Entering their synagogues, he preached, but his teachings were rejected. He moved to a different city, Anti-Anti, but again with the same results. He moved into the land of Middoni, but once more, few would believe.

Cast into prison, Aaron and his companions suffered great abuse, but their lives were preserved, and they were delivered through the missionary efforts of Ammon, Aaron's brother, and King Lamoni.

Aaron next proceeded to the land of Lehi-Nephi where he had unusual success and was able to teach and convert many thousands of Lamanites who became a righteous, peaceful, God-serving, and faithful people.

After returning to Zarahemla, not a great deal more is recorded of Aaron's life. Reference is made to his accompanying Alma to Antionum on his mission to the Zoramites, where they taught with faithful enthusiasm.

Though wayward and thoughtless as a youth, once convinced by the angel that God's work would prevail, Aaron was a changed individual, and he gave the Lord his undivided efforts to make amends for what he had done earlier.

Lamoni Is Converted

The transforming effect of the Gospel of Christ in a person's life is dramatically illustrated in the conversion of Lamoni, the Lamanite king over the land of Ishmael.

He was a convert of Ammon, one of the four sons of King Mosiah.

Prior to Ammon's coming, Lamoni was a ruthless monarch, governing the land of Ishmael under the supervision of his father who was sovereign over all the Lamanites.

Lamoni ruled his people harshly and wickedly, often executing a servant who was careless with the royal herds, permitting them to be stolen or plundered. Lamoni was totally ignorant of Christ, the Gospel, and even of his own heritage.

But Ammon, fasting and praying that he might teach the Gospel to Lamoni and his people, became a servant to the king, protected his property and through faithful service, converted Lamoni, his wife, the queen, and many of the servants and people.

The story of these conversions is a dramatic incident told in Chapters 18 and 19 of Alma, and illustrates the redemptive power of God. The episode ends with these words:

". . . they did all declare unto the people the self-same thing—that their hearts had been changed; that they had no more desire to do evil.

". . . and as many as did believe were baptized; and they became a righteous people . . . thus the Lord did begin to pour out his Spirit upon them: and we see that his arm is extended to all people who will repent and believe in his name."

Lamoni, now repentant of his former behavior, accompanied Ammon to nearby Middoni, to help free Ammon's three brothers who had been imprisoned for their preaching.

Enroute, they met Lamoni's father, who attempted to slay his son for having accepted the friendship of Ammon. But Ammon stepped between the father and son, overcame the angry emperor, and won from him complete liberty for the land of Ishmael.

After gaining the freedom of Ammon's brothers, Lamoni, with Ammon, returned to his homeland. Lamoni caused that the Church be established and that synagogues be built where the people could be taught the Gospel.

Lamoni told his people that they were free, no longer subject to the oppression of the Lamanite emperor, and that they "have the liberty of worshiping the Lord their God according to their desires . . ."

Thus Lamoni became an instrument in the hands of the Lord for doing great good among his people; and the people of Ishmael became "zealous in keeping the commandments of God."

Alma, The Younger

The pre-eminent man of his time, Alma, the Younger, as a youth, persecuted the Church. But an angel ordered him to cease.

"Why persecutest thou the Church of God? For the Lord has said: 'This is my Church, and I will establish it, and nothing shall overthrow it . . .'"

Converted not unlike Saul of Tarsus, Alma became presiding high priest of the Church, chief judge of the people, a mighty prophet, unyielding in his war on wickedness, a fervent missionary, an effective administrator and organizer of the Church an articulate teacher of Gospel principles, an unvanquished warrior, and triumphant commander.

Yet for all his honors and successes, he remained humble: "I have labored, even from the commencement of the reign of the judges until now, with mine own hands for my support . . ."

Alma's love was whole and vibrant as his prayer for the sin-wracked Zoramites shows: "Behold, O Lord, their souls are precious, and many of them are our brethren; therefore give unto us, O Lord, power and wisdom that we may bring these, our brethren, again unto thee."

Alma cried: "O that I were an angel, and could have the wish of mine heart, that I might go forth and speak with the trump of God . . . and cry repentance unto every people . . ."

He found comfort in the thought that his purpose was to urge men to seek righteousness; "I know that the Lord has commanded me . . . that perhaps I may be an instrument in the hands of God to bring some soul to repentance; and this is my joy."

Beautiful blessings were given by Alma to his sons, and with them he labored as a missionary, visiting cities, teaching, expounding, and admonishing adherence to the truth.

Near the end of his life, Alma, speaking to his beloved son, Helaman, summed up his life in these words:

". . . I have labored without ceasing that I might bring souls unto repentance; that I might bring them to taste of the exceeding joy of which I did taste . . .

"And I have been supported under trials and troubles of every kind, yea, and in all manner of afflictions; yea, God has delivered me from prison, and from bonds, and from death; yea, and I do put my trust in him, and he will still deliver me.

". . . and I will praise him forever . . ."

When he knew his end was near, Alma departed from Zarahemla and was never heard of again, which caused the belief to be widespread that the Lord had taken him, "even as Moses."

Amulek: Receives Call

The call to serve the Lord came to Amulek of Amonihah directly from an angel.

Journeying to visit a close relative, Amulek was accosted by a messenger of God, who told the wealthy, influential Nephite, ". . . return to thine own house, for thou shalt feed a prophet of the Lord; yea, a holy man, who is a chosen man of God . . . and he shall bless thee and thy house . . ."

The holy man was Alma, the Younger, whose appeals to the citizens of Ammonihah to forsake their evil ways and return to God fell upon deaf ears. In disappointment, Alma was leaving the city when an angel appeared to him also, and instructed him to return and continue his cries for repentance.

Amulek, obedient to the angel's instruction, returned home. Enroute he came upon Alma who invited him to his home, and was converted to the gospel.

"I never have known much of the ways of the Lord and his mysteries, and marvelous power," Amulek later testified, but through his association with Alma, he came to know the truth and labored valiantly the remainder of his life to teach the Gospel of Christ to his fellow Nephites.

The labor of missionary work, however, cost him dearly. He was cast into prison, abused, and saw the destruction of many who were burned because of their testimonies.

Finally, escaping from prison by the hand of God, Amulek and Alma abandoned Ammonihah to its fate—destruction by the Lamanites—and journeyed to the land of Zarahemla where they were successful in establishing the Church.

In leaving Ammonihah, Amulek forsook "all his gold, and silver, and his precious things, which were in the land Ammonihah, for the word of God, he being rejected by those who were once his friends and also by his father and his kindred."

But Amulek never lost his testimony, gained through Alma's friendship. Because of his faithfulness, Amulek taught many of the children of Lehi to walk in paths of righteousness ". . . having got the victory over the devil, and the word of God being preached in its purity in all the land, the Lord pouring out his blessings upon the people."

Judging from the sermons of Amulek, he appears to have been a man of broad education, unfaltering integrity, and of zealous faith. He was a man of affectionate character who became a favorite of Alma and accompanied this great Nephite prophet in many missionary ventures.

Amulek loved his family intensely, and had deep compassion for the faithful. Yet he loved the Lord more, and gave up all he had for the riches and happiness of the Gospel.

Corianton: A Wayward Son

Near the end of his life, Alma the Younger wrote letters to his three sons, Helaman, Shiblon, and the youthful Corianton.

The latter two had accompanied their father in his mission to the Zoramites. Corianton forsook his ministry "and did go over into the land Siron . . . after the harlot Isabel."

Alma admonished Corianton that his brothers had set a good example for him, that he was boastful of his own strength and wisdom, and that he failed to follow his father's teachings.

"Thou dids't do that which was grievous unto me," chastizes Alma, admitting that the unchaste Isabel "did steal away the hearts of many; but this was no excuse for thee," he adds.

"These things are an abomination in the sight of the Lord," warns Alma, adding, "Ye cannot hide your crimes from God; and except ye repent they will stand as a testimony against you at the last day."

Because of Corianton's behavior, Alma's mission was made especially difficult, and many Zoramites rejected the Gospel.

Corianton had additional shortcomings, and in his letter, Alma sought to clarify and teach his ill-informed son. Corianton believed his sins were justified because of God's mercy; he wondered why men should be informed about the coming of the Savior so far in advance; he worried about the resurrection, and the justice of God in punishing sinners.

Each of these problems is examined and explained by Alma in his counsel to Corianton in Chapters 39-42 of the Book of Alma.

The great prophet concludes his letter by urging Corianton to "let these things trouble you no more, and only let your sins trouble you with that trouble which shall bring you down unto repentence."

As a final word, he encourages Corianton to remember that he is called of God to preach the Gospel: ". . . go thy way, declare the word with soberness and truth, that thou mayest bring souls unto repentance."

That Corianton heeded his father's words is indicated in later passages: "The sons of Alma did go forth among the people, to declare the word unto them."

Alma gave the sacred records into the keeping of Helaman, the eldest son. Helaman passed them on to Shiblon, but when Shiblon prepared to die, he was unable to give them to Corianton—presumably he was worthy to become the custodian—because "he had gone forth to the land northward in a ship," and was heard of no more. So Shiblon gave the records to his nephew Helaman, named after his father.

Alma's instructions to Corianton indicate that salvation is a personal thing, and that though the son's wickedness was serious, through repentance he could hope for forgiveness and salvation.

Pahoran: Chief Judge

Pahoran had a communications problem with his chief general, Moroni.

As chief judge of the Nephites, Pahoran had lost his position and was forced to flee the royalists who preferred to be ruled by a king rather than a judge. In his deposed status, Pahoran was unable to aid Moroni in his wars with the invading Lamanites.

Uninformed of this situation, however, Moroni sent an angry letter to Pahoran charging him with a host of failures including neglect, thoughtless stupor, withholding arms, provisions and manpower, exceeding slothfulness, and even of being "traitors to your country."

Moroni called on Pahoran to repent and promptly send food and men to the war area that he might successfully continue the fighting in defense of freedom and liberty. If Pahroan should fail, warned Moroni, "I come unto you, even in the land of Zarahemla, and smite you with the sword."

The noble character of Pahoran is seen in his mild answer to the distressed general. "I do not joy in your great afflictions, yea, it grieves my soul," Pahoran wrote, explaining why he was unable to come to Moroni's help.

"You have censured me, but it mattereth not: I am not angry but do rejoice in the greatness of your heart. I, Pahoran, do not seek for power, save only to retain my judgment-seat that I may preserve the rights and liberty in the which God has made us free," he wrote, urging Moroni to come with a force and join him in driving out the King-Men and regaining the judgment-seat.

The message that Pahoran remained faithful and was still a freedom-loving patriot pleased Moroni. He rallied a force to join his friend, and together they recaptured the city of Zarahemla.

Most of Pahoran's rule was marked by war and strife. Immediately upon becoming chief judge, a rebellion broke out in which the royalists, preferring a king, refused to join in defense of their land and freedom from the invading Lamanites. Moroni was enlisted to put down the defections. The effects, however, were felt for years and the Nephites were left in a weakened condition to battle the Lamanites.

When the war finally ended, Helaman, who had been serving as one of Moroni's generals, and others, went among the people teaching, preaching, and restoring the Church. Pahoran spent his time restoring civil order to his land.

A wise public servant, Pahoran judged his people with courage, and exercised his powers in righteousness. He proudly demonstrated his loyalty, and his letter answering Moroni marks him as a patient, understanding, and forgiving leader.

Moroni: Mighty General

At twenty-five Moroni became supreme commander of the armies of the Nephites, and for eighteen years led them in battles and wars against the evil Lamanites.

Amalickiah, the Lamanite king, so came to hate Moroni because of his unending string of victories, that the wicked ruler swore to drink Moroni's blood. Instead, Amalichkiah died at the hand of one of Moroni's generals, Teancum.

Yet, during this same period, the Church prospered and grew under the leadership of Helaman, Shiblon, Corianton, Ammon, and others to such a degree that Helaman wrote:

". . . never was a happier time among the people of Nephi, since the days of Nephi, than in the days of Moroni . . ."

That this could occur despite the constant fighting is a mark of the high character of the general. Helaman describes him thusly:

"And Moroni was a strong and mighty man; he was a man of a perfect understanding; yea, a man who did not delight in bloodshed; a man whose soul did joy in the liberty and the freedom of his country, and his brethren from bondage and slavery;

"Yea, a man whose heart did swell with thanksgiving to his God for the many privileges and blessings which he destowed upon his people; a man who did labor exceedingly for the welfare and safety of his people.

"Yea, and he was a man who was firm in the faith of Christ, and he had sworn with an oath to defend his people, his rights, and his country, and his religion, even to the loss of his blood."

Such a man would be slow to anger, but when confronted with persecution and slavery, no man could withstand his righteous indignation.

To this great Nephite general probably goes the distinction of raising the first flag of liberty in the Western Hemisphere.

When he heard of the dissensions and rebellions among the Nephites, Moroni, in anger, tore apart his coat and wrote upon one piece:

"—In memory of our God, our religion, and freedom, and our peace, our wives and our children . . ."

This he fastened to a pole and called it the "title of liberty." Then bowing himself before the Lord, he prayed mightily for liberty to rest upon his people.

The faithful—identified as "Christians"—rallied to his support and promptly drove the dissenters from their midst.

One can but wonder what this liberty-loving patriot would think—and do—to those who desecrate and profane the banners of freedom in our day.

Downfall Of Amalickiah

Ambition—vain, inglorious, soul-destroying ambition—was Amalickiah's downfall.

Ambition made him a traitor, turning him against his own people, the Nephites.

Ambition led him to apostasy and rejection of the teachings of the Gospel.

This same gnawing ambition for power led Amalickiah to murder, to create endless war and destruction between the righteous Nephites and the wicked Lamanites.

Amalickiah was a descendant of Zoram, the servant of Laban. A brilliant officer in the Nephite armies, Amalickiah rejected the form of government (rule by judges as established by King Mosiah), and joined with the King-Men who gathered an army and elected him their general.

The more brilliant and righteous general, Moroni, however, gathered an even larger force, and Amalickiah fled to the Lamanites where, through murder, deceit, fraud and treachery, he became first their general and then their ruler.

Once king, Amalickiah's ambition grew to rule both Lamanites and Nephites—to reign from ocean to ocean. To accomplish this, he raised an immense army and set out to conquer the Nephites.

But the war was a disaster for the Lamanite forces, and the wicked monarch, in anger, cursed God and swore he would drink the blood of the victorious Moroni.

Again a huge army was raised, and this time the Lamanites were more successful, capturing many Nephite cities until they came up against the stalwart Nephite general, Teancum, and a corps of veteran warriors who brought the invasion to a halt.

Following a particularly vicious battle, Teancum slipped into the Lamanite camp at night, and finding Amalickiah in an exhausted sleep, drove a spear into his heart, thus ending an evil life.

In recording these events, Helaman writes that the Nephite dissenters who followed Amalickiah into the camps of the Lamanites had been taught righteousness.

". . . nevertheless, it is strange to relate, not long after their dissensions, they became more hardened and more impenitent, and more wild, wicked and ferocious than the Lamanites . . . yea, entirely forgetting the Lord their God."

Commenting upon the frailty and waywardness of men such as Amalickiah, Helaman writes:

"O how foolish, and how vain, and how evil, and devilish, and how quick to do iniquity . . . are the children of men" when they "set their hearts upon the vain things of the world."

The tragedy of Amalickiah's life is how much good he could have done had he been willing to follow the Lord.

Lehonti: Lamanite King

Three times the treacherous Amalickiah invited Lehonti to come down the mountain, and three times the chary Lehonti refused.

When Amalickiah finally went up the mountain and Lehonti agreed to a meeting near his camp, it was his undoing.

Lehonti came to power when the Lamanites were ordered to war against the Nephites. The king had been persuaded by the power-hungry and turncoat Nephite Amalickiah to go to war against the Nephites.

When the Lamanite king sent a call to arms proclamation throughout the land, the people were "exceedingly afraid." They were frightened of their king, but they feared even more the Nephites under their mighty general, Moroni.

The Lamanites refused to go to war, and the king, learning of the rebellion of his people, gave Amalickiah command of the remaining loyal forces and ordered him to force the people to arms.

When the fearful Lamanites saw Amalickiah's army approaching, however, they fled to Onidah—"to the place of arms."

So determined were they not to fight the Nephites that they organized themselves and appointed Lehonti, one of their officers, to be their new king and leader.

The people then gathered upon the top of a mountain called Antipas, ready to wage war with Amalickiah rather than fight the Nephites.

But Amalickiah wanted no civil war among the Lamanites. He had other plans. Instead, he camped at the bottom of the mountain and requested an audience with Lehonti. After Lehonti refused three times, Amalichiah went up the mountain and met his opponent.

The perfidious Nephite plotted to have the king's army surrounded by Lehonti's forces, and then surrender. In return, Lehonti would make Amalickiah his second in command.

Lehonti agreed to this high treason, and in the morning, Amalickiah's army, seeing itself surrounded, gave up rather than do battle with their own countrymen. As agreed, Amalickiah was named second in command.

But Lehonti had not reckoned fully with the cunning Amalickiah, for ". . . Amalickiah caused that one of his servants should administer poison by degrees to Lehonti that he died."

As was the custom, Amalickiah, second in command of the Lamanite army, then was appointed chief—the very thing he had schemed from the first.

Amalickiah was now able to dispose of the Lamanite king by outright murder, have himself appointed monarch, and caused great suffering and destruction among the Nephites.

Helaman Leads Armies

To Helaman we are indebted for the outstanding war story in the Book of Mormon, and one of the most faith promoting experiences in all scriptures.

Little is recorded of the personality of Helaman. But that he must have been a man of unusual persuasion, formiable faith, and of warm thoughtfulness is unquestionable.

Helaman was a high priest and loved to teach the principles of righteousness. He labored diligently to keep the Church organized following the death of his father, Alma, the Younger.

But wars led the mighty Moroni to appoint Helaman a general, and it is in this service we learn to know him best.

The invading Lamanites became such a threat to the Nephites that 2,000 Ammonite young men volunteered to join the Nephite armies if Helaman would lead them. One can only wonder at the love, respect, and faith they must have had for him.

In a letter to Moroni, Helaman details their battles: ". . . never had I seen such great courage." It was courage born of faith seeded in these 2,000 striplings by their mothers.

Before leading them into their first combat, Helaman asked them how they felt. Their reply:

"For as I had ever called them my sons (for they were all of them very young) even so they said unto me: Father, behold our God is with us, and he will not suffer that we should fall. . . .

". . . and they did think more upon the liberty of their fathers than they did upon their lives; yea, they had been taught by their mothers, that if they did not doubt, God would deliver them."

When the battle was over, Helaman fearfully called the roll: "But, behold, to my great joy, there had not one soul of them fallen to the earth; yea, they had fought as if with the strength of God . . ." he wrote.

In a subsequent battle, every one of the 2,000 were wounded, and 200 fainted from injuries and loss of blood. ". . . nevertheless, according to the goodness of God, and to our great astonishment, and also the foes of our whole army, there was not one soul of them who did perish . . . and we do justly ascribe it to the miraculous power of God because of their exceeding faith in that which they had been taught."

Following thirteen years of war, Helaman returned to the labors he loved best, teaching the Gospel and setting the Church in order. He had much success and received great joy because of the increased faithfulness of the people.

Helaman lived sixteen years after his father, Alma, during which time he also was keeper of the records. At his death, Helaman passed the records and "sacred things" to his brother, Shiblon.

Lehi II: Like Unto Moroni

As tragic, miserable, and horrible as war is, it sometimes has the paradoxical characteristic of bringing out the best in some men. One such was Lehi, a corps commander under the mighty general and leader of the Nephites, Moroni.

Almost all that is recorded in the Book of Mormon of Lehi's life is related to his military activities. Yet the record says of him that he was "a man like unto Moroni." One can only wonder what virtues marked his personality to cause the historian to pay him such high tribute.

Lehi may have been a son of Zoram; the record is not specific, but that he was a devoted and loyal commander to

Moroni is fully evident. As such he is an equal to Teancum, another close military, religious leader, and associate of Moroni.

Lehi first appeared as a Nephite general in a war with the Lamanites led by Zerahemnah. Moroni, through the use of spies and strategy, managed to trap the invading armies. He justified his actions in these words:

". . . it was the only desire of the Nephites to preserve their lands, and their liberty, and their church, therefore, he thought it no sin that he should defend them by stratagem . . ."

Lehi and his troops play a key role in the defeat of Zerahemnah, being the first to fall on the Lamanites and send them fleeing across the River Sidon into the waiting forces of Moroni. The war ended in complete victory for the Nephites.

Later, when the apostate Nephite, Amalickiah, began his wars against the Nephites, Lehi was again in high command, now as a chief captain of the city of Noah. This had been the weakest of Nephite fortifications, but Moroni, presumably aided by Lehi and his men, had strengthened the city with new defenses.

Thus when the Lamanites came against Noah, they discovered it was not only stoutly secure, but also that the Nephite leader was Lehi, and they were "again disappointed, for they feared Lehi exceedingly." The Lamanites lost more than 1,000 men, including all their captains; only fifty Nephites were wounded in an unsuccessful attempt to capture the city.

The fury and energy with which the Nephites battled are explained in Moroni's words:

"The Nephites were inspired by a better cause, for they were not fighting for monarchy nor power but they were fighting for their homes and their liberties, their wives and their children, and their all, yea, for their right to worship and their church."

The final reference to Lehi is found in Alma 53:2: "Now behold, this Lehi was a man who had been with Moroni in the more part of all his battles; and he was a man like unto Moroni, and they rejoiced in each other's safety; yea, they were beloved by each other, and also beloved by all the people of Nephi."

Teancum Loved Liberty

Teancum was a patriot. He loved liberty, his people, and his country, and fought with brilliant, uncompromising courage in their defense.

As one of Moroni's senior generals, Teancum was the leader of a corps of superior warriors who repulsed the invading Lamanite armies led by the traitorous Amalickiah.

". . . for every man of Teancum did exceed the Lamanites in their strength and in their skill of war, insomuch that they did gain advantage over the Lamanities."

To guide such troops, Teancum, himself, must have been a forceful and fearless individual, marked with unusual ability to inspire men to follow him into raging battles.

Teancum was personally daring in the defense of his people—to the point of being impetuous and even rash.

Angered by the ruin and ravages of the wretched Amalickiah, he sought out the mighty Lamanite king and slew him.

Following a harassing, day-long battle, both sides withdrew in fatigue. But Teancum, accompanied by his servant, "stole forth and went out by night, and went into the camp of Amalickiah . . . stole privily into the tent of the king, and put a javelin to his heart; and he did cause the death of the king immediately that he did not awake his servants."

Amalickiah was succeeded by his brother, Ammoron, who continued to occupy cities captured by the Lamanites. To lure them out of the fortified city of Mulek, Moroni had Teancum and his soldiers act as bait, enticing the invaders from the city with a chance for an easy victory. But Teancum led the Lamanities into a trap and Moroni and his forces destroyed them, recapturing Mulek in the process.

The fighting continued, however, and Teancum, angered again by the destruction of lives and property wrought by the arrogant Ammoron, attempted to repeat his daring feat by slipping into the enemy camp at night and killing the wicked monarch. Teancum slew the king, but lost his own life also.

Teancum's story in the Book of Mormon is limited to this seven-year period of war between the Nephites and Lamanites. The history, however, tells much about the character of this brave man.

He was courageous, loyal, and faithful. He was a skilled and resourceful warrior as well as gifted leader, and at his death, both Moroni and his fellow officers "were exceeding sorrowful."

In abridging the records, Mormon writes of Teancum:

". . . he had been a man who had fought valiantly for his country, yea, a true friend to liberty; and he had suffered very many exceeding sore afflictions."

Evil Ways Of Gadianton

Gadianton was an out-and-out monster, taught by "that same being who did plot with Cain . . . who spread the works of darkness and abominations over all the face of the land," namely Lucifer.

Desiring to be elected chief judge over the Nephites—promising his blackhearted associates places of high honor if he were—Gadianton conspired with another apostate, Kishkumen, to assassinate the chief judge, Helaman.

The attempted murder failed, however, and Gadianton and his followers fled into the wilderness where they became raiding bands of robbers and murderers, thereafter known as Gadianton Robbers.

As the people sinned, the bands grew in size and influence. At one point, they were able to gain control of the government and almost overthrow and destroy the Nephites.

Little is recorded about Gadianton himself, but we can deduce from the records that he was crafty, cunning, treacherous, and sinister. Mormon details the great evil that resulted from his conspiracy with Satan:

The secret oaths and covenants did not come to Gadianton from the records which were given to Helaman, "but behold, they were put into the heart of Gadianton by that same being who . . . is the author of all sin."

Gadianton, and those who succeeded him, carried on "the works of darkness and secret murder and . . . handed down plots and their oaths and their covenants and their plans of awful wickedness, from generation to generation. . . ."

Invariably, wherever they gained a foothold, these conspirators wrought destruction and ruin. When they could not gain control by legitimate means, they murdered. At one time, so great had they become in numbers that the righteous Nephites and Lamanites were gathered on one side and warred with the Gadiantons on the other.

Readers of today's news will recognize in the world existence of men with the same vile intentions—to murder, plunder, rob, destroy freedom, and persecute righteousness.

Writing to readers today about secret combinations, Moroni warned:

"And whatsoever nation shall uphold such secret combinations, to get power and gain, until they spread over the nation, behold, they shall be destroyed;

"Wherefore, the Lord commandeth you, when ye shall see these things among you that ye shall awake to a sense of your awful situation, because of this secret combination which shall be among you. . . .

"For it cometh to pass that whoso buildeth it up seeketh to overthrow the freedom of all lands, nations, and countries, and it bringeth to pass the destruction of all people, for it is built up of the devil, who is the father of all lies. . . ." (Ether 8:22)

Lachoneus: Man Of Faith

Mormon, in writing of Lachoneus and his troubled reign as chief judge of the Nephites, describes him as a "just man." He was that and more: he was courageous, and a remarkable leader of unusual persuasion. Above all, he had great faith.

As leader of the Nephites, he saw his people being pillaged and persecuted by the Gadianton Robbers. So brazen had the robbers become that their evil leader, Giddianhi, wrote an insolent letter to Lachoneus demanding that the Nephites surrender and join the Gadiantons—or perish.

Lachoneus ignored the arrogant idea, and instead, "did cause that his people should cry unto the Lord for strength against the time that the robbers should come down against them."

In addition, he sent a proclamation among the people urging them to gather together with all their possessions in a central place where they might unitedly stand firm against the forces of evil. Obediently, the Nephites followed Lachoneus' instruction, and he taught them to repent and cry unto the Lord that they might be delivered.

"So great and marvelous were the words and prophecies of Lachoneus that they did cause fear to come upon all the people, and they did exert themselves in their might and do according to the words of Lachoneus."

Well organized, fortified, and supplied, the Nephites were filled with courage from the teachings of Lachoneus, and his chief general, Gidgiddoni. When the Gadianton Robbers finally came to battle, they were utterly routed and their leader, Giddianhi, was slain.

A second time the robbers threatened Lachoneus and his people, this time with siege. But so secure were the Nephites that the Gadiantons themselves suffered from lack of food and constant counter attacks until they admitted failure and began a withdrawal.

But Gidgiddoni, learning of the retreat, sped an army through the night to block escape. The Gadiantons, facing superior forces both front and rear, were defeated a second time.

The Nephites spent several more years living together in harmony and strength before they felt secure enough to return to their former homes and cities.

Eventually they did spread throughout the land again, however, with peace and prosperity their lot. A period of rebuilding occurred, and cities and highways were constructed or repaired under Lachoneus' leadership.

For a short period, the people remained humble, obedient, and grateful to God for his preserving and protective strength. But they were unable to withstand the temptations of wealth and the vain things of the world. Soon they were "led away . . . to do all manner of iniquity."

Giddianhi The Robber

Though he is described as bold, Giddianhi also was insufferably arrogant. He was chief and general of the Gadianton Robbers in the days shortly preceeding the visit of Christ to the Nephites.

Signs of the birth of the Savior had been given the people, but in a very short period many had fallen into great wickedness. Many went over to the Gadianton Robbers, who became strong and fearless, causing misery and destruction among the righteous.

So bold were the robbers that Giddianhi sent an insolent letter to Lachoneus, the Nephite governor, saying:

"It seemeth a pity unto me that ye should be so foolish

and vain as to suppose that ye can stand against so many brave men who are at my command . . ."

". . . because of the many wrongs which ye have done unto them . . . I write unto you desiring that ye would yield up unto this my people, your cities, your lands and your possessions . . . and unite with us and become acquainted with our secret works, and become our brethren and that ye may be like unto us—not our slaves . . ."

The evil robber signed his name: "I am Giddianhi; and I am the governor of this the secret society of Gadianton; which society and the works thereof I know to be good; and they are of ancient date and they have been handed down unto us."

Lachoneus was "exceedingly astonished" to receive the letter, but he "was a just man, and could not be frightened by the demands and threatenings of a robber."

So powerful had the robbers become, however, that Lachoneus gathered the righteous, with their flocks and possessions, into a central, united force. But rather than yield, he organized the people, called them to repentance, and prepared them for war.

The action proved disastrous to Giddianhi and his army. When they came out of the wilderness and mountains where they lived, they discovered the Nephites had abandoned their lands and cities.

Soon, starvation began to threaten Giddianhi and his troops, and they knew they must defeat the Nephites to survive. Dressing themselves with lambskins about their loins, shearing their heads, and painting themselves with blood, the robber army marched.

Lachoneus and his people, seeing the robbers approach, fell to earth in prayer asking God to preserve them in war. But the Gadiantons, thinking their appearance had frightened the Nephites, gave a loud shout and stormed to battle.

". . . Never," writes Moroni, "was known so great a slaughter among all the people of Lehi since he left Jerusalem . . ."

The robbers were defeated, and Giddianhi, "who had stood and fought with boldness, was pursued as he fled; and being weary because of his much fighting he was overtaken and slain. And thus was the end of Giddianhi the robber."

Hagoth: A Curious Man

Hagoth is mentioned in the Book of Mormon only once by name (Alma 63:5). Yet the reference to him is important:

"And it came to pass that Hagoth, he being an exceedingly curious man, therefore he went forth and built him an exceedingly large ship . . . and launched it forth into the west sea, by the narrow neck which led into the land northward."

The next several verses tell how other expeditions of Nephites sailed off "with much provisions, and also many women and children."

Hagoth also built other ships. Some voyages were successful and made return trips; another ship "also did sail forth;

and whither she did go we know not," according to Shiblon, who kept the records.

Tradition has it that some of the ships that did not return may have reached the islands of the Pacific—the Hawaiian Islands, the Society Islands, the Samoan Islands, and Easter Island. If so, natives of these islands may be descendants of the Nephites.

The possibility that ships could sail and drift west across the Pacific Ocean was demonstrated in 1946 by the Norwegian ethnologist, Thor Heyerdahl. He was also a "curious man," built a raft of balsam logs, named it *Kon-Tiki,* and drifted west from Gallao, Peru, 4,300 miles to the Raroia Islands.

In 1969 Heyerdahl built a raft of papyrus and sailed from the northwestern coast of Africa to the Western Hemisphere. His purpose has been to demonstrate the possibility of Near Eastern peoples migrating to the American continents by drifting and sailing boats.

What kind of ships Hagoth built is, of course, unknown. But that he must have been a skillful mechanic and master builder can be appreciated. His crafts carried "many" Nephites, and they were sufficiently seaworthy to make return trips.

It is generally assumed the voyagers who traveled "to the land northward" probably landed somewhere along the California coast. Hagoth's ship was built "on the borders of the land Bountiful, by the land Desolation," and the "narrow neck" that led northward may have been what is now the area of Panama.

Hagoth is described as "exceedingly curious." This characteristic is in keeping with the spirit of the Gospel. To be curious is to want to learn, to gain knowledge. The late Albert Einstein, scientist, said of curiosity:

"The important thing is not to stop questioning. Curiosity has its own reason for existing. One cannot help being in awe when he contemplates the mysteries of eternity, of life, of the marvelous structure of reality. It is enough if one tries merely to comprehend a little of this mystery every day. Never lose a holy curiosity."

Hagoth, the Nephite ship builder, had such curiosity.

Samuel The Lamanite

He was a stranger in their midst, accusing them of evil, warning that unless they turned to God and kept His commandments, they would surely perish.

Such intemperate words by a Lamanite angered the sin-minded Nephites, and they drove the preacher, whose name was Samuel, from their city, Zarahemla.

Feeling that he had failed in his mission, Samuel decided to return to his own people—the Lamanites, who were living obediently because of the teachings of Nephi and Lehi, sons of Helaman.

The voice of the Lord came to Samuel, however, and told him to go again to Zarahemla and prophesy to the people the feelings of his heart.

Upon returning, Samuel was denied entrance at the city gate, so he climbed upon the wall and from there, in a loud voice, began preaching to the people.

Among the extraordinary things he predicted were that within five years the Savior would be born into the world— that a great light would appear at his birth, and at his death, darkness would engulf the earth—and that within 400 years, except they repented, the entire Nephite nation would perish.

"And now . . . If they will not repent, and observe to do my will, I will utterly destroy them, saith the Lord, because of their unbelief notwithstanding the many mighty works which I have done among them . . ."

The people were enraged and tried to stone Samuel, but to no effect. They shot arrows at him, but the protecting power of God was around him, and he could not be harmed.

Then the people became alarmed, and cried to their captains, "Take this fellow and bind him, for behold, he hath a devil; and because of the power of the devil which is in him we cannot hit him with our stones and our arrows; therefore take him and bind him, and away with him."

But Samuel jumped down from the wall and fled into his own land and was heard no more by the Nephites.

The things Samuel prophesied came to pass. A few believed his words, and sought out Nephi, and were baptized. More believed later when the signs he forecast came to pass at the time of the Savior's birth. The greater part of the people of Zarahemla would not repent, however, and eventually perished.

When Jesus appeared to the Nephites as the resurrected Christ, He asked why the prophecies of Samuel the Lamanite were not written on the records. "How be it that ye have not written this thing . . . And it came to pass that Jesus commanded that it should be written."

Samuel, courageous, obedient, faithful, and compassionate, spent the remainder of his life teaching his own people, the Lamanites.

Helaman II: A Noble Man

For about 470 years of Book of Mormon history, the Gospel was taught from father to son in an unprecedented succession of leadership.

Their names are in an unusual order: Alma the Elder, Alma the Younger; Helaman, the son of Alma, Helaman, the son of Helaman; Nephi, the son of Helaman, Nephi, the disciple, the son of Nephi, and Nephi IV; Amos, the son of Nephi, and Amos, the son of Amos.

Each of these remarkable men successively presided over the Church and had charge of the sacred records.

Helaman II, who comes half way in this extraordinary list of fathers and sons, was as outstanding and unusual as his fore-bearers and descendents.

The Book of Mormon reads, "He did keep the commandments of God, and did walk in the ways of his father." Of his two sons, Nephi and Lehi, the scribe has written, "they began to grow up unto the Lord."

In addition to being presiding officer of the Church, Helaman II also was elected by voice of the people to fill the judgment-seat. Yet almost as soon as he assumed office, the Gadiantons plotted to seize power.

Kishkumen, an assassin, "sought to destroy Helaman," and enroute to commit the murder met a servant of Helaman who knew the robber society's secret signs and oaths. The servant learned of Kishkumen's evil mission and "as they were going forth unto the judgment-seat, did stab Kishkumen even to the heart, that he fell dead without a groan."

The servant hurried to inform Helaman of the plot, and he sent forces to capture the Gadiantons, but they sensed when Kishkumen failed to return that something had gone wrong, and escaped into the wilderness.

During Helaman's reign, the Nephites multiplied and spread across the entire Western Hemisphere, building temples, synagogues, cities; they also engaged in extensive ship building. Moroni writes that they kept "many records," which were "particular and very large," and that his account does not contain "a hundredth part of the proceedings of this people."

"Helaman did fill the judgment-seat with justice and equity, yea, he did observe to keep the statutes, and the judgments, and the commandments of God; and he did do that which was right in the sight of God continually; and he did walk after the ways of his father, insomuch that he did prosper in the land."

There was continued peace, despite the Gadiantons, and thousands "joined themselves unto the Church and were baptized unto repentance."

So great was the growth of the Church and the blessings poured upon the people, "that even the high priests and the teachers were themselves astonished beyond measure."

Nephi II: Few Greater

So great was Nephi's sorrow, when he returned to his home in Zarahemla after a preaching tour in the North and found his people living in wickedness, that his heart was broken.

From a tower in his garden, this son of Helaman poured out his soul to God:

"Oh, that I could have had my days in the days when my father Nephi first came out of the land of Jerusalem . . . then would my soul have had joy in the righteousness of my brethren."

Nephi's prayer was overheard, and when he arose and saw a crowd had gathered, he preached to them with deep conviction, rebuking them for wickedness, and exhorting them to repent.

But there were unbelievers in the crowd who needed proof. Nephi gave it to them in a testimony: they would find the chief judge dead upon the judgment-seat. So it was! But Nephi was accused of the deed, since he seemingly knew about it. The real murderer, however, was identified by Nephi and confessed, whereupon the prophet was set free.

So unusual were these events that people gathered in groups on the streets and argued about them. Nephi was left alone. As he turned, downcast and dejected, to his home, the Lord spoke to him.

Nephi was commended for his faithfulness: ". . . blessed art thou, Nephi, for those things which thou has done; for I have beheld how thou hast with unweariness declared the word . . . and thou has not feared them, and has not sought thine own life, but has sought my will, and to keep my commandments."

For this the Lord covenanted in the presence of angels; "I will bless thee forever; and I will make thee mighty in word and deed, in faith and works."

Nephi was given power over the people, the elements, to seal and to loose, and bless and curse. He also was promised protection from harm.

Strengthened by this wonderous witness, Nephi continued preaching, and when his message was rejected and people sought to seize him, "the power of God was with him, and they could not take him to cast him into prison."

Nephi served as chief judge, but after nine years, because of the people's wickedness, he gave up the judgment-seat and spent the remainder of his life teaching the Gospel. In many of these labors he was accompanied by his brother, Lehi, and together they brought thousands to an understanding faith.

With Lehi, Nephi stood unharmed in the midst of fire from heaven. He lived with God, and his life testifies of conspicuous faith, courage, humility, compassion, and patience. Few prophets are greater. Two of his sons, Nephi and Timothy, were chosen by the Lord to be his apostles.

Nephi the Disciple

Nephi was troubled. Samuel the Lamanite had prophesied that signs would be given to the people of the birth of the Savior.

Those who spurned such teachings, however, "began to say the time was passed" for his words to be fulfilled, and "they did make a great uproar throughout the land" and even set a deadline after which those who yet believed would be put to death.

Nephi, son of Nephi, grandson of Helaman, high priest and prophet of the Nephites ". . . went out and bowed himself down upon the earth and cried mightily to his God in behalf of his people . . ."

Nephi prayed all day, and God answered him:

"Lift up your head and be of good cheer; for behold, the time is at hand . . . and on the morrow come I into the world . . ."

Many of the Nephites were now converted when they saw the signs that night—there was no darkness and a new star appeared in the heavens—and Nephi went among the people teaching and baptizing.

Nothing specifically is recorded of Nephi's life for the next thirty years. There was peace, then contention, more peace and prosperity, and then gradually the people became ripe in evil.

Finally, Nephi appeared again, this time boldly proclaiming the Gospel, calling the wayward to repentance. Moroni records that Nephi was visited by angels and the voice of the Lord; "and Nephi did minister with power and great authority."

Next is recorded the destruction of the wicked. Then follows the most dramatic event recorded in the Book of Mormon: the appearance of the resurrected, glorified Christ (III Nephi, Chapter 11) to the Nephites.

Jesus organized his Church and appointed twelve disciples the first of whom was Nephi. The twelve were commanded to baptize the people. Nephi himself was the first to be baptized in this new era ushered in by the Savior. The senior disciple then baptized the remaining eleven.

As they came out of the water "the Holy Ghost did fall upon them . . . they were encircled about as if with fire . . . and angels did come down out of heaven and did minister unto them."

During the days the Master spent with the Nephites, He taught them the precious and joyful truths of His gospel, many recorded in this book which bears Nephi's name (III Nephi).

Following the departure of the Savior, Nephi continued to lead the people. He gave care of the records to his son, Nephi. Another son, Jonas, was one of the twelve disciples.

What kind of high character Nephi—the disciple—must have had can only be marveled at when it is considered that he was chosen leader of his people when the resurrected Redeemer revealed himself to the Nephite branch of the House of Israel.

Nephi IV: Holy Man

Almost nothing is recorded of the personality of Nephi IV, a son of Nephi who was a son of Helaman, a son of Alma, the Younger.

From what is written, however, Nephi IV must have been a man of noble and holy character.

He was a young man when the Christ appeared to the Nephites. His father, Nephi, was selected as the first of the Twelve Disciples (Apostles) by the Savior.

Shortly after the Savior's visit, Nephi IV was charged with keeping the sacred records and plates of the Nephite people. He retained them in his possession for seventy-six years, until his death, when they were given to his son, Amos.

Why Nephi III did not keep the records and sacred things is not disclosed. Possibly as head of the Twelve, and leader of the Church, the responsibility was given to his son in order that the father could administer the affairs of the Church—indeed, of the whole people and land, for the period that followed the Messiah's appearance is known as the golden era of Nephite history.

In abridging the records, Mormon summarizes the period, 258 years—of which Nephi IV serves the first seventy-six—in eighteen verses.

Surely, great events must have occurred following the Savior's mission. Yet we are told only that the Church was organized in all the lands round about, that everyone, Lamanites and Nephites alike, were converted, and war and contention ceased.

The people held all things in common for the first 167 years; every man was just and equally treated; there were no rich and no poor; all were loved and blessed equally of the Lord.

Great and wonderous works were performed by the Twelve Disciples; they healed the sick, raised the dead, caused the lame to walk, and the deaf to hear.

The Nephites became "exceedingly fair and delightsome," multiplying and filling the land with a strong and mighty race.

Mormon records:

"And there were no envyings, nor strifes, nor tumults, nor whoredoms, nor lyings, nor murders, nor any manner of lasciviousness; and surely there could not be a happier people among all the people who had been created by the hand of God.

"And how blessed were they! For the Lord did bless them in all their doing . . ."

The period was a taste of the millennium to come, perhaps, and this may be why Mormon was constrained to make his abridgement so brief—that the holiness of the period not be revealed to later generations.

Presuming Nephi IV to be the chief spiritual guide and leader of his day, we can only wonder at what a godlike personality he must have been to head such a righteous people.

The Brother Of Jared

The Brother of Jared was a large and mighty man, highly favored of the Lord.

His name, said the Prophet Joseph Smith, was Mahonri Moriancumr. It is not given in the Book of Mormon.

No man of greater faith has walked the earth. He said to the Mountain Zerin, "Remove—and it was removed."

He pleaded with the Lord that his language—the pure language of Adam—might be preserved, and the Lord personally led him and his people away from the confusion of tongues at the Tower of Babel.

No man received greater spiritual manifestations than those given the Brother of Jared, wrote Moroni, who abridged and translated his voluminous writings. So beautiful and powerful were the Jaredite records that Moroni, writing in the language of the Nephites confessed to his own ineptness.

Once, when Mahonri Moriancumr failed to call upon the Lord for four years, the Almighty appeared unto him in a cloud and chastened him for three full hours. ("For whom the Lord loveth, He chasteneth . . .")

Once, the Brother of Jared asked the Lord to put light in stones, and the veil was removed from his eyes, and he saw the finger of the Lord.

So shaken was he by this experience that he fell to the earth in surprise, and when the Lord asked him why, he explained he did not know the Lord had flesh and blood and feared he would be struck.

Never, said the Lord, had man come before him with such faith. Did he see more than this? He asked.

"Nay," answered the Brother of Jared, "Lord, show thyself unto me." The Lord then made himself manifest in the spirit and told Mahonri Moriancumr that because of his faith which had brought to him this knowledge, he was redeemed of God.

"Never have I showed myself unto man whom I have created, for never has man believed in me as thou hast," the Lord said.

The Lord then "ministered" unto the Brother of Jared "even as he ministered unto the Nephites." What this was we know only briefly, for at one point in Mormon's record of the Savior's visit to the Nephites, he wrote:

"The eye hath never seen, neither the ear heard before, so great and marvelous things as we saw and heard Jesus speak . . . and no tongue can speak, neither can there be written by any man, neither can the hearts of men conceive so great and marvelous things as we both saw and heard Jesus speak . . ."

The Brother of Jared led his band of people to the Western Hemisphere where they soon created a mighty civilization. When he died, full of years and honor, he left a posterity of twenty-two sons and daughters.

Coriantumr: A Willful Ruler

The story of Coriantumr is one of a willful, despotic ruler determined to hold on to his power. The end result was total destruction of his people.

Coriantumr was king of the Jaredites and sovereign over all the land. Despite their heritage, the Jaredites had forsaken the Lord.

The Prophet Ether warned them that unless they repented, they would be completely destroyed. If they would turn from their wicked ways, they would be spared.

Ether added a fearful warning to Coriantumr that he would be the last to remain alive and would see the utter annihilation of the once noble race. He also would see another people possess the land, established by heaven to be a land of freedom to those who would serve the Lord.

Though a potent ruler, artful in the ways of the world, and skilled in the warrior's trade, the sinful Coriantumr ignored Ether's prophecy.

Within a year of Ether's warning, however, rebellion broke out, and from then until the end of his days, Coriantumr knew little but the devastation and horrors of war. In one particular round of battles, writes Ether, two million men were slain.

If the wives and children of these men also died in the fighting—there is reason to believe they did—surely it must have been the bloodiest fighting in the world's history.

So great was the slaughter, that even the unregenerate king sickened and wrote to his enemy, Shiz, offering to give up the kingdom if the fighting would cease.

But the grossly depraved Shiz, having placed himself in the hands of Satan, agreed only if Coriantumr surrendered to be slain.

Coriantumr refused, and the battles began anew with victories going first to one side, then to the other. Hate and desire for vengeance grew until eventually, during a four-year standoff, both sides marshalled all their forces for one conclusive, deadly campaign.

When the fighting finally began, every man, woman, and child in the land was enlisted.

After two days, so many had been slaughtered that Coriantumr again wrote Shiz and offered to yield up the kingdom if the people were spared. Again Shiz refused.

Finally, after eight days, all except Coriantumr and Shiz were dead. The Jaredite king rested on his sword for a bit, records Ether, then smote off the head of the vindictive Shiz who had fainted from loss of blood.

Thus Ether's prophecy was fulfilled: the Jaredites were utterly destroyed.

Coriantumr lived for some time, wandering alone across the ravaged land. Eventually he stumbled into an unknown people, the Mulekites, with whom he lived for nine months before dying.

Shiz: A Brutal Man

Shiz was an altogether brutal, savage, and cruel man. The military commander who fought against Coriantumr and his faction of the Jaredites, Shiz was viciously vengeful.

He became general of the dissident Jaredites when his brother, Lib, was killed in a battle with Coriantumr. So enraged was Shiz that he routed Coriantumr and his forces, savagely pursuing them from the Plains of Agosh to the seashore.

The chase was ghastly as Shiz and his army obliterated and annihilated everything and everyone in their path to the sea. So fearful and terrible was the destruction that the saying swept the land, "Who can stand before the army of Shiz? Behold, he sweepeth the earth before him!"

So furious was Shiz in his spirit of murderous revenge that he swore to have Coriantumr's blood. When the two armies finally came together, Shiz threw his forces against Coriantumr in three consecutive days of horrifying destruction. On the third day, Corintumr was wounded, fainted from loss of blood, and was carried from the battlefield as though dead. But Shiz' forces had so spent themselves they could not pursue their advantage and broke off the engagement.

Two million people were destroyed in these running battles, according to Moroni's abridgement of the Jaredite record.

When Coriantumr recovered from his wounds, he remembered the prophecies of Ether that the Jaredites would be destroyed unless they repented. Coriantumr wrote to his adversary and offered to give up the kingdom if the people would be spared.

But the vengence-bent Shiz replied that only the life of Coriantumr would satisfy him. Coriantumr refused to give himself up, and the wars began anew.

First the victory would go to Coriantumr, then to Shiz. Finally, the two sides gathered for a struggle of extermination at the Hill Ramah. Day after day the fighting raged until one night there remained of the entire race of Jaredites thirty-two people of Coriantumr, and twenty-nine of Shiz.

Then, all but the two generals were dead. Now, Shiz fainted from loss of blood. Coriantumr rested upon his sword for a while, then "smote off the head of Shiz."

Literally millions of people—men, women, and children—died in the wars of these two willful men who must go down in history as ruthless and bloodthirsty and who fought only for power.

The Jaredites were mighty warriors. Moroni, in his condensing the original text, writes: "And they were large and mighty men as to the strength of men." Coriantumr and Shiz must have been of such physical character to be their leaders.

But they were weak in their faith in God and His works, rejecting the dire predictions of the prophets, and Shiz, particularly, gave his soul over to a passion for murder that has few equals.

Ether: Jaredite Prophet

For a year, Ether had hidden in a cave, fearful for his life, coming out only at night to observe the destruction of the Jaredite people because of their wickedness.

Now the word of the Lord came to Ether. He was instructed to go to the king, Coriantumr, and prophesy that unless he repented—he and his household—he and all his people would be destroyed.

Ether promised Coriantumr that if he did repent, the Lord would give him a kingdom and spare the people. If he could not refrain from evil, Coriantumr would live to see the total destruction of the Jaredites.

The wicked king would not repent, nor would his people, and they sought to kill Ether. Again, Ether hid himself in a cave from where he saw within a few years the fulfillment of the Lord's word.

Ether was the last prophet of the Jaredites—and a particularly fine scribe—to whom we are indebted for the record of the Jaredites, an abridgement of which was made by Moroni and is known as the Book of Ether in the Book of Mormon.

Ether was of a royal race, descended from Jared. Favored of the Lord, Ether was given vision of the full history of the earth, from Adam to the end of time.

The Jaredite people would not listen to Ether's appeals for righteousness—any more than they heeded the words of prophets who preceded him. When the Jaredites finally grew weary of his preaching, they drove him from their midst. He hid himself in "the cavity of a rock" and would come out at night to view the course of events he knew would inevitably come to pass.

While so hidden, he wrote the history of his time year by year, and watched the people gradually destroy each other in unrelenting warfare.

So great was the bloodshed and destruction that several times even the evil Coriantumr plead for mercy from his enemies that the fighting might cease.

When the annihilation was over, the Lord "spake unto Ether, and said unto him: go forth, and he went forth and beheld that the words of the Lord had all been fulfilled, and he finished the record."

In abridging the record enscribed on twenty-four plates of gold, Moroni writes ". . . and the hundredth part I have not written."

Ether then hid the record "in a manner that the people of Limhi did find them" while searching for the land of Zarahemla.

Now alone, yet faithful and humble, Ether concludes his history: "Whether the Lord will that I be translated, or that I suffer the will of the Lord in the flesh, it mattereth not, if it so be that I am saved in the kingdom of God."

Ammaron: Record Keeper

Ammaron was a librarian whose responsibility was to keep the sacred treasury of religious and secular writings of the Nephites.

He was a young brother of Amos, who cared for the records for an amazing 112 years. The father of these two long-lived men also was called Amos. He kept the records for eighty-four years, receiving them from his father, Nephi, son of the first disciple named by the Savior when he visited the Nephites.

The writings of Nephi, Amos, and his sons, Amos and Ammaron, covering 320 years, are briefly abridged by Mormon into a single four-page chapter of forty-nine paragraphs.

Ammaron kept the records about fifteen years, and then "being constrained by the Holy Ghost, did hide up the records which were sacred . . ."

Ammaron, aged himself, then appointed Mormon, only ten years old, to be custodian, telling him he had hidden the treasury in a hill called Shim, in the land of Antum.

Mormon was instructed to observe all things concerning his people and after he was twenty-four years of age, to write on the plates of Nephi what he saw.

How many records Ammaron hid "unto the Lord" is not related, but they included the Small Plates of Nephi, the Large Plates of Nephi, the Plates of Ether, and a translation of these latter-plates made by King Mosiah. From these various records, plus the brief but important writings of Mormon and his son, Moroni, comes our present edition of the Book of Mormon.

Additional items possibly preserved by Ammaron might have been the Brass Plates and Sword of Laban, the Liahona, and the Urim and Thummim.

The Small Plates of Nephi contained the unabridged writings of nine men: Nephi, Jacob, Enos, Jarom, Omni, Amaron, Chemish, Abinadom, and Amaleki, and compose the first 131 pages of the Book of Mormon.

These Small Plates were made by Nephi about thirty years after Lehi and his party left Jerusalem. Recorded on the plates were the sacred writings of the Nephites—prophecies, commandments, and the work of the prophets and their testimonies.

The Large Plates of Nephi were made before the Small Plates, shortly after Nephi arrived on the Western Continent. Written on these plates was the secular history of the people. When the Small Plates were filled, scribes used the Large Plates to record both the secular and religious history of the Nephites.

Abridged by Mormon from the Large Plates are writers in five books, Mosiah, Alma, Helaman, III Nephi, IV Nephi, and his own writings. These books take 338 pages in the present edition.

Also abridged, by Moroni, were the twenty-four plates of Ether, giving a brief history of the Jaredite nation.

After giving his instructions to the boy Mormon, Ammaron is heard of no more. We can only surmise he was a faithful, obedient servant of God, sensing the sacred nature and vital importance of the records entrusted to his care.

Mormon Engraves Plates

All of his life, Mormon knew war, strife, and contention. At one time, his people became so degenerate that he refused to lead them. So wicked were they that the Lord even forbid Mormon to preach to them.

He must have been a remarkable youth. At ten, he was given care for the records and was told to engrave on the plates of Nephi everything he observed concerning his people.

At fifteen, he was visited by the Lord so that he "tasted and knew of the goodness of Jesus."

In his sixteenth year, he "did go forth at the head of the armies" of the Nephites against the Lamanites.

At twenty-four he acquired the records which had been hidden for safe keeping. He kept them in his possession until shortly before his death, at about seventy-five when he delivered them to his son, Moroni.

In the intervening years, Mormon led his people in one continual round of war against the Lamanites and the Gadiantons.

In these wars, first one side would win, then the other. The result was pillage, cruelty, bloodshed, woe, and ever-increasing hatred.

Reveling in their undeserved victories, but declining to be grateful to the Lord for their preservation, the Nephites grew more wicked until finally, Mormon would not take responsibility for them any longer and refused to lead them.

Finally, when depravity reached its vilest level, both Nephites and Lamanites enlisted every man into two vast hordes and met in a battle of total destruction at the Hill Cumorah. When the fighting ended, the victorious Lamanites had killed all but twenty-four Nephites, including Mormon and Moroni. Later, Mormon was slain by a Lamanite.

It is as a chronicler and historian that we recognize Mormon's conspicuous character.

He compiled and abridged the records delivered to him by Ammoran, and for this the entire record bears his name. In addition, one book within the volume also carries his name.

In his own record, Mormon writes that he was "a sober child," and "quick to observe." When appointed general of the armies, he wrote: "And notwithstanding I being young, was large in stature, therefore the people of Nephi appointed me . . . their leader."

We recognize in the personality of Mormon a righteous, formidable leader, skilled in the art of war, but also taught "after the manner of learning of my people," a faithful defender of the teachings of the Redeemer, and a devoted father.

Shown in his writings also is his great compassion for his people. He wrote:

"And my soul was rent with anguish, because of the slain of my people, and I cried:

"O ye fair ones, how could ye have departed from the ways of the Lord!

". . . Behold, ye are fallen, and I mourn your loss. O that ye had repented. . . ."

Moroni Ends Record

In November, 1831, Joseph Smith received a revelation from the Lord which, in part, reads:

"O inhabitants of the earth, I have sent forth mine angel flying through the midst of heaven, having the everlasting gospel . . . who shall appear unto many that dwell on the earth."

The angel was Moroni, who was given jurisdiction of the sacred records by his father, Mormon.

The appearance of Moroni to Joseph Smith was in fulfillment of John's vision as recorded in Revelations:

"And I saw another angel fly in the midst of heaven, having the everlasting gospel to preach unto them that dwell on the earth . . ."

Moroni was the last representative of the Nephites, and he witnessed their total destruction as an officer under his father. As custodian of the records, Moroni hid them in the earth—the Hill Cumorah—to prevent them from falling into the hands of the Lamanites who, he wrote, would have destroyed them.

When it was time for the Prophet Joseph to receive the plates for translating, Moroni counseled him that he should take every precaution to protect them:

"The same heavenly messenger (Moroni) delivered them up to me with this charge: that I should be responsible for them; that if I should let them go carelessly, or through any neglect of mine, I should be cut off . . ."

Later, the Prophet explained, "They remained safe in my hands, until I had accomplished by them what was required at my hand. When . . . the messenger called for them, I delivered them up to him; and he has them in his charge until this day . . ."

Moroni wrote upon the plates that his entire people were destroyed, "and I even remain alone to write the sad tale . . . And whether they will slay me, I know not. Therefore I will write and hide up the records in the earth; and whither I go it mattereth not."

A few paragraphs later, however, Moroni wrote that he had again taken up writing in the records, after a period of twenty years, during which time he apparently wandered across the American Continent in hiding and fear of the Lamanites.

Moroni completed the record of his father, denouncing the wicked generation that would be in the world when the Book of Mormon should come forth. He also warned and exhorted men to be faithful.

Closing his father's record, Moroni then abridges the twenty-four plates containing the record of the Jaredites, known as the Book of Ether. After this, he added "a few more things, contrary to that which I had supposed; for I had supposed not to have written any more." Added are ten chapters of his own history, instructions, teachings, and letters of his father, and his own final compassionate farewell to the Lamanites.

These chapters show Moroni to be a man of noble character, an obedient son honoring his father, and a faithful servant of God.

Oliver Cowdery:
The Second Elder

"... we have seen the plates ... they have been translated by the gift and power of God ... we have seen the engravings which are upon the plates ... we declare with words of soberness that an angel of God came down from heaven, and he brought and laid before our eyes, that we beheld and saw the plates ... we bear testimony."

To these plain and simple words of witness are signed three names: Oliver Cowdery, David Whitmer, and Martin

Harris. They are known as the "Three Witnesses." Their testimony prefaces each copy of the Book of Mormon.

Of the three men, Oliver was closest to the Prophet Joseph Smith.

He was Joseph's scribe and wrote nearly all of the translation of the Book of Mormon as it fell from his lips.

Oliver himself, received the gift of translation. With Joseph, he received the keys of the Aaronic Priesthood.

The first man baptized in his dispensation, Oliver, again with Joseph, received the Melchizedek Priesthood from Peter, James, and John.

When translation of the plates was completed, Oliver saw to its publication. He was one of the six original members of the Church, and was ordained the "Second Elder" by the Prophet.

The first public sermon given by a member of the Church was delivered by Oliver Cowdery. He was one of the first missionaries of the Church.

He was the first editor of the *Evening and Morning Star,* was a member of the first high council of the Church, and with Joseph, was the first to covenant to pay tithing.

Oliver was a member of the School of the Prophets, and, as one of the Three Witnesses, helped select the first Twelve Apostles in this dispensation.

He was appointed an assistant counselor to the President of the Church, Joseph Smith, in 1837.

Yet despite all of this privileged work, Oliver found fault with the Prophet Joseph, fell from select positions, and was separated from the Church.

For ten years, the disaffected Oliver remained severed from the Church, practicing law in Ohio and Wisconsin.

But during this period he remained steadfast in his resolution that the Book of Mormon was true scripture.

Finally, humbling himself, and asking for forgiveness of the Saints, he was rebaptized, and planned to cross the plains and join with the Church. Before this occurred, however, he suffered an infection and died.

David Whitmer:
Testified He Saw

To David Whitmer we are indebted for a fascinating description of how the Prophet Joseph Smith translated the golden plates.

"He (Joseph) had two small stones of a chocolate color, nearly egg shaped, and perfectly smooth, but not transparent, called interpreters, which were given him with the plates. He did not use the plates in the translation, but would hold the interpreters to his eyes and cover his face with a hat, excluding all light, and before his eyes would appear what seemed to be parchment, on which would appear the characters of the plates in a line at the top, and immediately below would appear the translation, in English, which Smith would read to his scribe, who wrote it down exactly as it fell from his lips."

David Whitmer then explains how the scribe read the sentence back to the Prophet, and if mistakes had been made, the characters from the plates would remain before his eyes until the translation was written correctly.

Then the line would fade and another line would appear.

Shortly before the translation was completed, David, with Oliver Cowdery and Martin Harris—the Three Witnesses —were shown the plates by an angel according to instructions Moroni had written in his abridgement of the writings of Ether:

"And behold, ye may be privileged that ye may show the plates unto those who shall assist to bring forth this work; and unto three shall they be shown by the power of God . . ."

David Whitmer was rightly qualified to become one of the witnesses of the work. He had aided the Prophet and his family during the translation period, some of the actual work being done in the Whitmer home. Some of the hand-written "printer's manuscript" of the Book of Mormon is in the handwriting of Christian Whitmer, David's brother.

David Whitmer was one of the original six members of the Church. He became a leading figure, was ordained a high priest, became president of the first high council, and, as one of the Three Witnesses, helped select the Twelve Apostles of this dispensation. In 1834, he was ordained to be Joseph Smith's successor.

David became discordant with Church leadership, however, and in April, 1838, was excommunicated by the high council at Far West. He lived another 50 years, never rejoining the Church, but whenever challenged, reaffirming his testimony:

"I have never at any time denied that testimony, or any part thereof . . ." he said near the end of his life.

"As sure as the sun shines and I live, just so sure did the angel appear unto me and Joseph Smith, and I heard his voice, and did see the angel standing before us . . ."

David Whitmer was accepted by family and friends as an honest, conscientious, and upright man, open and frank, and well-respected in Richmond, Ray County, Missouri, where he remained after leaving the Church.

Martin Harris:
A Faithful Witness

One hundred years ago William Harrison Homer was returning from a mission to Great Britain. He stopped to visit the Kirtland Temple and there found his sister's father-in-law, Martin Harris, eighty-six, acting as a guide.

When asked about his testimony of the Book of Mormon and Joseph Smith, the frail little man, bent with age and disappointment, answered fervently:

"Young man, do I believe it! Do I see the sun shining! Just as surely as the sun is shining on us . . . just as surely as the breath of life sustains us, so surely do I know that Joseph Smith was a prophet of God, chosen of God to open the last dispensation of the fulness of times; so surely do I know that the Book of Mormon was divinely translated. I saw the plates; I saw the angel; I heard the voice of God. I know that the Book of Mormon is true and that Joseph Smith was a true prophet of God. I might as well doubt my own existence . . ."

Martin was born at Easton, Albany County, New York, in 1783. When ten, he moved with his family to near Palmyra. Here he remained until 1831, a prosperous farmer and trustworthy citizen.

On occasion he hired Joseph Smith Jr. to work on the farm. Martin took keen interest in Joseph's story and in 1827, gave him $50 to assist "in doing the Lord's work." Martin also acted as scribe for a short period of Joseph's translation work.

In 1829, in an act of remarkable generosity, Martin mortgaged 240 acres of his farm for $3,000 to finance publication of 5,000 copies of the Book of Mormon. He was one of the first to be baptized into the Church when it was formally organized in 1830. Martin also accompanied the Prophet to Missouri in 1831, taking part in dedicating Jackson County as the gathering place for the Saints of Zion.

In February, 1834, Martin Harris was named a member of the Kirtland High Council. A year later he joined Oliver Cowdery and David Whitmer in selecting and ordaining the first council of the Twelve Apostles—an assignment given to the Three Witnesses.

Active and faithful until the majority of members moved to Missouri, Martin remained at Kirtland. He became disassociated with the Church, and in December, 1837, was excommunicated.

Elder Homer, returning to Salt Lake City, reported his conversation to Brigham Young. A short time later, Edward Stevenson was authorized to raise funds to bring Martin Harris to Utah. He arrived August 30, 1870, and was reconciled to the Church, rebaptized and spent the last few years of his life energetically bearing his witness of the divinity of the Book of Mormon.

A few hours before his death, at 92, he said:

"I know what I know. I have seen what I have seen and I have heard what I have heard. I have seen the gold plates from which the Book of Mormon is written. An angel appeared to me and others and testified to the truthfulness of the record . . ."

Joseph Smith:
A Modern Prophet

The day had been cold and the members of the Twelve had spent most of it meeting at the home of Brigham Young in Nauvoo, Ill.

Now, as he made his way in the dark over the frozen ruts in the street to his own home, Joseph Smith reflected on the activities of the day. The meeting had been good, and he was encouraged. Joseph Fielding had returned from a four year mission to England and reported success.

Later, the Prophet wrote in his history under the date Sunday, November 28, 1841:

"I spent the day in the council with the Twelve Apostles at the house of President Young, conversing with them upon a variety of subjects . . . I told the brethren that the Book of Mormon was the most correct of any book on earth, and the keystone of our religion, and a man would get nearer to God by abiding by its precepts, than by any other book."

If any man knew this to be a fact, Joseph Smith Jr. did. As a boy, he had been visited by God the Father, and his Son, Jesus Christ. He had been given the gold plates by Moroni, an angel, and by the power of God, the plates had been translated. These two events had formed the warp and woof of his life.

The Book of Mormon was "most correct." Joseph knew. "Through the medium of the Urim and Thummim I translated the record, by the gift and power of God." Such a claim could be made for no other book on earth.

With insight, Joseph used the word *keystone* to describe the importance of the Book of Mormon. A keystone is the highest, the crowning point of an arch, regarded as binding the whole together. So the Book of Mormon! As the Angel Moroni had told him: ". . . the fulness of the everlasting Gospel was contained in it, as delivered by the Savior to the ancient inhabitants." Without the Book of Mormon, Joseph Smith understood, the Saints would not have the Gospel, correct and in its entirety.

Its "precepts" did bring a person "nearer to God," Joseph knew. He had lived the precepts himself. The book's purpose was to "show unto the remnant of the House of Israel what great things the Lord hath done for their fathers; and that they may know the covenants of the Lord, that they are not cast off forever—and also to the convincing of the Jew and Gentile that Jesus is the Christ, the Eternal God, manifesting himself unto all nations . . ."

The Prophet Joseph Smith brought forth the Book of Mormon as a new witness that Jesus Christ is the Son of God, the Redeemer of the world, the Christ, the eternal God, and that He lives.

From the hour he walked from the Sacred Grove after being visited by the Father and the Son in 1820, until he was shot and killed twenty-four years later by a painted-faced mob, Joseph Smith so testified.

Jesus The Christ

The dominant figure of the Book of Mormon is Jesus Christ, the Redeemer of the world, the Son of God the Father.

The Book of Mormon is a witness—a testimony—to the world to the reality of Jesus Christ: That He lives!

The prophets of the Book of Mormon testified that the Christ would come into the world in the flesh, that He would lay down His life to redeem mankind, and that He would break the bands of death through resurrection. They taught that all who would follow after Him would gain salvation.

Both before and after His Advent, Jesus manifest himself to those in the Book of Mormon who were of great faith, notably, the Brother of Jared, Lehi, Nephi, Alma, Ether, and others.

The Father, in a dramatic presentation, personally introduced the Risen Christ to the Nephites after his crucifixion:

"Behold, My Beloved Son, in whom I am well pleased, in whom I have glorified my name—hear ye him."

As He stood in the midst of the Nephites, the Savior stretched forth his hand and said:

"Behold, I am Jesus Christ, whom the prophets testified should come into the world; and behold, I am the light and life of the world; and I have drunk out of the bitter cup which the Father has given me, and have glorified the Father in taking upon me the sins of the world, in the which I have suffered the will of the Father in all things from the beginning."

Upon hearing this, the multitude fell to earth, realizing that God stood before them.

Jesus spoke again: "Arise and come unto me . . . that ye may know that I am the God of Israel, and the God of the whole earth, and have been slain for the sins of the world."

While among the Nephites, Jesus organized His church and taught the people the principles of the fullness of the Gospel. He performed miracles, healing the sick, casting out devils, and raising the dead. He administered the emblems of the sacrament, and in one glorious manifestation so holy the scribe was forbidden to write of it in detail. The Savior and His angels blessed and ministered to the children of the Nephites:

". . . and he took their little children, one by one, and blessed them, and prayed unto the Father for them . . . and they saw angels descending out of heaven as it were in the midst of fire; and they came down and encircled those little ones about, and they were encircled about with fire; and the angels did minister unto them."

Among the names used in the Book of Mormon for Jesus Christ are Mediator, Messiah, Lamb, Son of Righteousness, Son of the Eternal Father, Only Begotten of the Father, Creator, King of Heaven, Most High God, Lord Omnipotent, Mighty God, Holy One, Wonderful Counselor, Prince of Peace, and Jehovah.

In conclusion, we quote Nephi: "And as the Lord God liveth, there is none other name given under heaven save it be this Jesus Christ, of which I have spoke, whereby man can be saved."

Index

Savior, 16, 17, 23, 51, 70, 75, 80, 81, 82, 83, 85, 92, 105, 107.
School of the Prophets, 99.
Second Elder, 99.
Seer, 38.
Sherem, 16, 17.
Shiblon, 50, 51, 54, 61, 73.
Shilom, land of, 25.
Shim, hill, 93.
Ship, 9, 51, 72, 73.
Shiz, 87, 88, 89.
Sidom, 36, 37.
Sidon, river, 63.
Siron, land of, 50.
Smith, Joseph Jr., 3, 15, 84, 96, 97, 99, 100, 101, 102, 103, 104, 105.
Snow, Erastus, 15.
Society Islands, 73.
Son, the, 105.
Son of God, 105, 106; — of Righteousness, 107; — of the Eternal Father, 107.
Spirit, 3, 11, 29, 45.
Stevenson, Edward, 103.
Sword of Laban, 22, 93.
Synagogues, 43, 45, 77.

—T—
Teancum, 54, 57, 63, 64, 65.
Temple, 22, 26, 77.
Testimony, 49, 51, 98, 101, 102.
Thief, 10.
Three Witnesses, 99, 101, 103.
Timothy, 79.
Tithing, 99.
Title of Liberty, 55.

Tower of Babel, 84.
Twelve Disciples (Apostles), 82, 83, 99, 101, 103, 104, 105.

—U—
Urim and Thummin, 38, 93, 105.
Utah, 103.

—V—
Valparaiso, Chili, 3.

—W—
Western Continent, 93.
Western Hemisphere, 3, 4, 7, 9, 55, 73, 77, 85.
Whitmer, Christian, 101.
Whitmer, David, 98, 100, 101, 103.
Wild beasts, 15, 27.
Wisconsin, 99.
Wonderful Counselor, 107.
Word, the, 51.

—Y—
Young, Brigham, 103, 104, 105.

—Z—
Zarahemla, 21, 22, 24, 25, 31, 33, 34, 35, 36, 38, 41, 43, 47, 49, 53, 63, 74, 75, 78.
Zedekiah, 21.
Zeezrom, 36, 37.
Zeniff, 21, 24, 25, 33.
Zerin, mountain, 84.
Zion, Saints of, 103.
Zoram, 12, 13, 15, 59, 62.
Zoramites, 41, 43, 47, 51.